MAMA NEEDS A REFILL

MAMA NEEDS A REFILL

Finding Light in the Midst of Madness

Jenny Gwinn McGlothern

YOKE & ABUNDANCE PRESS

MAMA NEEDS A REFILL

Finding Light in the Midst of Madness

ISBN   979-8-88926-754-6   *Paperback*

979-8-88926-755-3   *Ebook*

To my Robbie, Maggie, and Simon.

Team Family on three.

CONTENTS

———

There is nothing to pour if your Cup is empty.

This is your invitation to refill.

INTRODUCTION

———

Dear Reader,

I thought becoming a mom would solve all my problems. Instead, having children became an excuse to avoid all the things about myself I didn't want to look at. I was raised by a mentally ill father and eventually a single mother, and I knew I wanted to raise my kids differently than my experience. I didn't know saying yes to parenting would bring up unresolved emotions from my own childhood. I didn't know that eventually, I couldn't run from my emotions anymore, and they would become gifts for me to open.

Parenthood isn't a job. It's a lifetime relationship. An adventure that never ends. In the over twenty-one years of being a mom thus far, the madness isn't only the constant busyness and caring for others, the groundhog days of the younger years, or the pushback of the teenage years; the madness is all of it. It's figuring out the evolving relationship with my children right alongside my own discovery and personal growth. I had a hard time when our kids were little because I didn't know who I was. I had stuffed down my drama and trauma from my past, and I thought being a mom was all I was cut out to do. When being a mom became difficult, I thought I was doing it wrong. I was challenged again when my children became young adults, and the world became tougher to navigate—eroding, exploding, and turning in what feels like a wrong direction. Along the way, I lost myself, found myself, lost myself, and found myself again and again. In building the relationships with my children, I discovered who I am and who I want to continue to become. As I continue to care for others, I am 100 percent clear it is vital and absolutely necessary to be awake to myself.

The madness is actually my invitation.

WHAT THIS BOOK IS AND IS NOT
This is not a parenting manual. The only parenting guide I wish I would've had would be instructions on how to care for myself first. This is a handbook for any relationship, an invitation to navigate life by starting with yourself.

When you start with you, you're actually supporting everyone more effectively. This book teaches you how to begin with yourself. When you do, you will discover this results in a loving ripple spreading out to everyone in your world. You will ignite deeper connection and avoid unnecessary drama—not all, for what is life without a bit of drama?

Keep in mind chaos, demands, emotional reality, mess, and struggle will still be part of your story, but now you will have inspiration and tools to help you navigate your road ahead. The hungers you have, when met, can even lead to you being more present in all your relationships. There is a way to honor yourself if you're willing to be curious and to surrender what that looks like.

This book is about how to pause and refill as you juggle it all. The fuel you will uncover is similar to the oxygen mask you are taught to put on first when flying on an airplane. Your fuel is lifesaving, and I will show you how to discover your own unique fuel and create time to actually use it.

Understandably, we can get lost, forget who we are, how we got here, what we are doing, and where we want to go. Good news: Your lifeboat comes from inside of you, it's accessible, and it's already here.

Holding a full Cup is being tuned into and fueled by your individual needs so that when it feels like all hell is breaking loose, you're supported. I have been someone who has lost it—my shit, my temper, my mind, my focus, and my identity—not only while raising our two children, while living this life. Discovering my anchors and utilizing them brought me back to shore.

While the world is recovering from a pandemic, falling apart in many ways, you can still find your footing and not be swept away in the madness. While those you love are going through a storm, you don't have to get blown away.

Let's make your support feasible and realistic for where you are right now. If you think pausing to attend to your needs sounds like something you can only get to in the distant future, I will show you another way. I will show you how pausing gives you more time and energy and is an incredible tool for your back pocket. I'm handing you a hall pass, some relief, and sustenance on your path.

My hope is a bit of my personal story, my experience as a life coach and creator of the sack-lunch-mini-retreat, becomes your inspiration, your nudge to fuel up in a way you had no idea could make such a profound difference.

YOUR STORY—YOUR CUP

Your "Cup-care" is vital to your well-being. I'm talking about your soul, your essence, that part of you that truly matters, and I refer to it as your metaphorical Cup. Your Cup is constantly talking to you, providing you support and guidance. When the nudges of help are ignored, you aren't the only one who pays with exhaustion or frustration—everyone around you pays. Your Cup offers you a guiding hand when, for the one-hundredth time, you are putting away toys, arguing with your teen, feeling unworthy, or pulling out your hair.

This loving inner voice from your metaphorical Cup has your back. When ignored, this is the part of you that leaves you feeling empty and wandering, lost and confused. When listened to, this is the part of you that guides you home.

For me, when our children were little, I ignored the nudges of meditation, practicing yoga, or getting outside for a moment to pause. My refusal to refill affected my entire family. I had nothing left to give—tank empty, spun out of control, and definitely not my best self. Everyone breathed in the noxious air and exhaled the toxicity.

Your Cup might say, *Yoo-hoo, over here! Pay attention. It's time for some sustenance.* It may whisper with repeated visits that at first seem like a distraction or crazy fantasy. My Cup had to swear like a sailor to get my attention. *Sit the fuck down and read your book!*

I felt as if my **soul and Spirit combined forces** by using my own vernacular to get my attention.

There are three ways you can establish your parenting mode of operation. The first is the same as you were raised. It's what you know. Your parents' mode of operation worked for you, and you want to pass on the great feelings you experienced. The second method is to raise your kids exactly the opposite way you were raised because you want them to have a different experience. You don't want them to feel what you felt. Or you can navigate as you go and **ask**, notice, stay present, and ask them again what they need from you. Your children will respond according to how they are wired, despite all the control you think you have over the situation.

PIECES OF MY STORY

The memories I do have from my childhood involved closed doors. My dad in his bedroom, sitting in his green pajamas and turning the ceiling yellow with his cigarette smoke. I was in my bedroom, staying out of everyone's way, talking to my stuffed animals, and playing in my fantasy world. In my bedroom is where I prayed to the God on the crucifix above my bed to cure my dad of his perpetual sadness. When I was on the other side of the door and my mom saw me crying, she would ask, "What's wrong?"

I shrugged my shoulders. Not wanting people to ask, my smile turned into my disguise. It was much easier to not explain what I was feeling, let alone figure out what I was feeling. This morphed into me finding it easier to take care of others than to take care of myself. Unaware of my needs, I allowed the needs of others to overshadow my life and take center stage.

In my thirties, before my husband and I decided to start a family, the one thing I absolutely knew I wanted to do with my life was to be a mother. I poured my entire being into being a mom to our children. When you don't process emotions, they eventually find you. My unhappiness and overwhelm of being a mother had nothing to do with being a mom to our kids but had everything to do with not processing my childhood and not learning how to be in touch with or express my feelings.

My unhappiness had everything to do with not making my feelings a priority or giving them any breathing room. I had ignored my needs for too long. In my forties, I had what I refer to as my first midlife crisis, without the affair or cherry red convertible. During this spiritual wake-up call, I redefined the definition of God I had grown up with, and that was no longer serving me. I began to question everything with the curiosity of a child. I found Spirit to be a concrete support and guide, living both outside of me and within.

Similar to the solace I found in my bedroom as a little girl, I was discovering strength and guidance both from Spirit and inside of me. At this time, I also found a meaningful career beyond motherhood and started my own life coach and retreat business, illustrating that we teach what we most need to learn. I discovered yoga, meditation, my community, and most importantly, my truth.

In my early fifties, it was time for my second spiritual crisis, still without an affair or shiny new toy. Therapy helped me unravel and understand my habits, reactions, triggers, ways of being, and easily distracted wiring. I uncovered the root cause of being unfocused and not living the dreams I, as a life coach, helped others live.

For a very long time, I used my kids needing me as an excuse to not discover myself. Their lives were right in front of me, and I assumed it was being a mom that was bumming me out. Because they were my focus, shoving any feelings around my own upbringing under the carpet was a lot easier. I got stuck in not knowing what I even wanted or desired. I was taught that life was my cross to bear; exactly the opposite of what I want to teach my children.

There is no magic pill to avoid feeling empty. However, when you tap into your intuition, resources, and answers waiting within, you receive useful navigation.

I recall the time when the only thoughts in my head were about how different I thought the whole motherhood thing would be. In the midst of raising our children, one March morning circa 2007, I balanced on one foot as I put the other into my jeans and yelled at the kids.

"Grab your backpack! Finish breakfast! Don't forget your coats! Hurry up! Don't bug your sister! Leave your brother alone! We need to be in the car in five minutes!"

I didn't like who I had become, and my yelling during the morning's madness was interrupted by the conversation I was having in my head. I heard the still small voice within, *Write a book and call it* Mama Needs a Refill. At that time in my life, I thought for sure it was God.

I have since deciphered this whisper to be coming from my soul, my Cup—the dwelling place of love, personal truth, and wholeness. The place beyond ego and personality. If you believe in God, this is one of the places I believe God resides. If you don't believe in God or are not sure if you believe in a Higher Power, I only offer these labels. You can always choose your own. I don't want the label of God to confuse, confine, or alienate but rather invite you further within yourself. I believe your Cup and Spirit is the juice of your knowing, the secret ingredient. My hope is the relationship you have with the part of you no one can see becomes your closest ally, your cherished friend, the one you seek out in the storm. Your Cup is a mystery and, like Spirit dwells within my Cup, I believe Spirit—a loving energy—dwells within yours. We are all worthy of this indwelling.

When I was frustrated about not knowing how to uncover joy in the challenges of motherhood, I wanted to escape. I saw escaping as the only option to healing my emptiness. I learned there was another option: soul care. By learning to listen and honor my Cup, I didn't walk out on my marriage or my children. I turned inward. This is where I found my wholeness. This is where I found help. This is how I didn't abandon myself.

Before taking care of everyone else, what will it take to give yourself permission to trust in the value of receiving support?

You may very well be juggling a number of balls in the air. Your time is precious. I've structured the book to get you the information needed for a particular moment, depending on your challenge, season, or stage of your adventure.

Each chapter is numbered as a "sip" and is a specific *invitation* toward a particular topic. The topics are listed in the "Table of Contents" for the fifty-six "sips." The "Refill Reflection" is food for thought. Morsels for action. If these exercises feel heavy, give yourself permission to come back to them at a better time.

When you see Cup, capitalized, I am referring to your soul.

May the pages in this book nudge you to honor your authentic fuel as you commit to nourishment that feeds your body, mind, and spirit. May you receive what you are looking for as you recognize the vital necessity of loving yourself.

Cheers, Jenny

PART ONE

TRUST

As you go about taking care of everyone, I bet you hear a voice coming from within. Often more than one. Your own mother's voice telling you what you should do. Your inner critic, insisting you're doing it wrong. The ego who often shouts its pessimistic views, distracting you from trusting your sixth sense. The voice I am inviting you to create a relationship with, learn how to trust, and to tune in to, some call Spirit, the still small voice within, or intuition. I call it the part of you that matters most, for it is the home of your knowing, your essence. Your soul's guidance. **I call it your Cup.**

This voice is the part of you that goes beyond your head, thoughts, and personality. It is the heart and innermost self, vying for your attention and wanting to escort you home. Home is your personal place of wisdom, love, and truth. You may internally scream for the whispers of your Cup to shut the F up, as they say something like, *Read that book; go for a run; take a break; learn how to meditate; rest a moment.* You couldn't possibly go for a run or sit down to breathe. But the whispers are your saving grace.

These whispers are your own wisdom wanting desperately to help you as you carry the weight of the world on your shoulders. Wanting to relieve you as you juggle all your responsibilities. Listening to these prompts from your soul will help you unlock what you need to learn, unlearn, and release. You are called to surrender to what is absolutely vital, no matter what stage of life you are in—a single mom, an empty nester, or with no kids at all and caring for elderly parents and the rest of the world. **Loving yourself is vital.** And loving yourself doesn't mean not loving your family and those you care for—**loving yourself *is* loving your family** and those you care for.

The voice from your Cup is the part of you that whispers to you in the dark, urging you to sit up, pay attention, and respect what is mumbled in your ear. Your Cup's voice arises to your conscious while you're driving down the highway or having a minute to yourself in the shower. This gentle speaker is not the critical, nasty voice distracting you, keeping you in resistance, and making you wrong. The voice from your Cup is the honest one that sometimes has to cuss to get your attention. This voice is both part of you and beyond you, often needing to sound like the way you would speak to be heard. This voice wants you to remember who you are before the dishes are done, exhaustion has settled in, or there is another meltdown—yours or someone else's. Your Cup is the container of your soul. The big, powerful, and essential part of you that you try to ignore because you have mouths to feed, hands to hold, and other's lives to care for. I invite you to trust this wisdom. Learn how to hear what your Cup is really saying as you listen to it.

Caring for your Cup is about listening to what it needs, nurturing its longings, and blessing your life by honoring its wisdom. Yes, in the midst of holding up everyone else. Most especially in the midst of the madness. When you lean into caring for your Cup and create a life-giving relationship through honoring this wisdom, you will discover its guidance is your trusted source, your ally.

SIP 1.

YOU FIRST

———

*Often mistaken as selfish, making
yourself a priority is vital.*

"Ha! Put me first?" you might exclaim. "Show me how putting myself first is possible with a baby attached to my breast, a toddler attached to one hip, a demanding job, a husband who is always out of town, a teenager who hates me, a dog that needs to be let out, and a parent who has moved in?"

Why is making yourself a priority vital? Because it changes everything. As you notice, believe, and learn to accept you are priority number one, this care and attention will ripple out to your family. When my children were little, I was certain taking care of their needs first made me a better mom. This left me depleted and dizzy. When they were teens, I was reminded again that the best way to connect with and support them was by attending first to my own unique fuel. I was a better listener after time for myself first. I was definitely kinder and had a greater capacity for patience and compassion.

Why does **doing for myself first not equate to ignoring others?** I show up better. Showing up for me results in showing up better for others. When I'm not fueled, they are the receiver of my underlying resentment and frustration. I don't have to say anything. They feel it.

When you suffer, they suffer. This translates to when you win, they win.

How is this possible? I learned that waiting after making their breakfast or after they were off to school never happened. I was invited to discover what oxygen best fueled me and how to best dispense its rejuvenating goodness. I got creative. I learned I had to start my day with *one thing.* I had to stake my claim that I'm indeed a priority. Creating time for myself was the difference between night and day. This is not an exaggeration.

One day, I found myself in tears on the kitchen floor. I decided to skip fueling up that day. Taking time for myself didn't seem important. I told myself I would do it later. I started off at full steam ahead, making lunches, solving problems, and answering demands—caring for everyone's needs but my own. I waited too long. I waited until I was having my own tantrum on the floor. Depleted.

And no, a shower, brushing your teeth, and cramming down an energy bar is not the same as making yourself a priority. Making yourself a priority and putting yourself first can look like this: You discover the small acts that not only fuel you but also satisfy a deep longing within and create positive results. Then you practice them regularly. You know how to do these small acts, and they're readily available first thing when you wake up, even if a kid wakes you.

Here are some bits of fuel that work for my clients, retreat attendees, and myself:

- stretch (release tight muscles)
- yoga (warrior pose for strength)
- breathe (deep inhale and exhale)
- meditate
- get grounded, feel your feet on the floor, and tell yourself something kind
- sit in silence with a mug of your favorite hot drink
- write in your gratitude journal
- draw a sketch in your art journal
- quiet time to plan your day
- note your day's intention on a whiteboard
- text a friend
- exercise
- pray
- step outside, hands outstretched, and thank the day
- sing with the birds
- thank the trees
- connect with self: with a hand on your heart, whisper a loving message

All these examples can be reduced to short-sweet-simple or extended for the occasions you allow and dedicate more time.

I discovered that with my short attention span, sitting up in bed for a short meditation, two stretches, one yoga pose, and writing down three words in my journal all **refill, anchor,**

and nourish me. Doing these activities sets the tone for the day far better than scrolling through social media or making the bed. When pressed for time, all these exercises can be included and done in under ten minutes. A handful or two of minutes are my saving grace.

Ten minutes for four things that didn't have to wait until the end of the day. Put clearly, ten minutes for me before anything else.

REFILL REFLECTION:

- Set the stage for the day.
- Give five minutes of your energy, attention, and time first thing in the morning to yourself.
  - Start your day of caring for others fueled up.
- Begin with one thing a day that's for you and put it at the top of your list.
- Treat this thing for you like an appointment you have on your calendar.
- No excuses, guilt, or blame.
- Participate in that one thing, knowing it nourishes your soul and provides you with the ability to be your best self.
- How can you simplify your action while still having it feed you?
- Fill your Cup.

SIP 2.

YOUR BREATH

———

Breathe the way you want to feel. This is your gift to open.

"Hello, ma'am. May I please speak to Mrs. McGlothern?"

The telemarketer wouldn't take my no to mean no.

I was making my daughter a tuna fish sandwich and had no patience to listen to what the telemarketer was selling. I slammed down the phone and proceeded to hyperventilate. The bowl of tuna was in my hand one moment and thrown against the wall the next.

Panic attacks don't look and feel the same for everyone. In the middle of my first panic attack, at the age of thirty-five, I believed I was going to die. I ran into the bathroom. Ringing in my ears, racing heart, and struggling to breathe. My husband gently handed me a paper bag and suggested I try to breathe into it. I may have thrown the bag at him.

Even though I couldn't catch my breath, what got me out of that moment was remembering I could breathe. Breathing is something I do every day without putting any effort into it.

While you go about your day and on through the night while you sleep, your breath keeps going. **Your breath is yours without asking.** When you intentionally and purposefully pause to get in touch with your breath, you will notice it slows you down, landing you into the present moment. (Try it now as your mind races, because you're reading this, to the laundry that is not getting done or the phone call you promised to make.)

Notice the dust settle around you. Come home to yourself with even one inhale and exhale. What you're thinking takes you out of the present moment. I will teach you other ways of getting present in subsequent sips, but for now, the most important tool to start with is the one that is yours for free. Your gift to open anytime, anywhere. Your breath.

If you've been holding your breath or hyperventilating, conscious breathing brings you to your center. **Your breath is your touchstone—your saving grace.** Conscious breathing has the incredible gift of calming you down, helping you focus and realign all parts of your being—body, mind, and spirit. Freaking out with worry, being overwhelmed, future-tripping, and panic can disappear as you become grounded in the present moment, one breath at a time.

Inhale.

Exhale.

The physical action of getting in touch with your breath slows you down and wakes you up to what is in front of you. Your breath, whether in the middle of a panic attack, looking for lost car keys, or driving carpool, brings you back to Earth.

Let's open your gift now.

OPENING YOUR GIFT:
- Eyes opened or closed, stop where you are, and inhale one big breath through your nose with your mouth closed.
- Hold your breath at the top of your lungs for three seconds if you can.
- Slowly exhale through your nose with your mouth closed.
- Repeat.
- If you're still here, commit to five breaths. Slow, intentional breaths. Observe each inhalation and exhalation. No need to force anything. Simply notice and be aware. Afterward, pay attention to how you feel.
- Still committed? Still breathing? This is an open invitation to come back to your breath and open the gift of presence one more time before the end of your day.
- Need a visual reminder? Move a piece of jewelry from the hand or wrist you normally wear it on, to the opposite hand or wrist. Write *breathe* on the back of your hand with a Sharpie or write it on the bathroom mirror in red lipstick. Add a reminder to your phone.

What if you did this exercise in between moving from one activity, responsibility, or commitment to the next? What if you decided to breathe the way you want to feel? Your breath is always available. Pull over, step away, be where you are, or lock yourself in the bathroom and breathe.

I learned from my first panic attack, which had me scared and throwing things, that once I stop trying to control my breath, it finds its own natural rhythm. If you aren't sure how to even allow your breath to find its own rhythm, know you can get to the place where you actually breathe the way you want to feel. Getting to this place takes intention and repetition. Keep showing up to your breath.

Perhaps you learned in yoga class about ujjayi breathing, where you breathe in and out through your nose, or the three-part breath to increase oxygen supply and calm your mind. There are many wonderful, helpful breathing techniques with fancy, hard-to-pronounce names you can learn in a class or from a Google search.

Don't make it complicated; breathe. No particular pattern, style, or rhythm but your own. As you relax into your breath, you become open to possibilities. If you were previously standing in confusion, notice how you feel now after intentional breathing. Instead of your thoughts of overwhelm or worry driving you all over the map, your breath becomes a guide you can trust. The natural healing properties of your breath calm, soothe, and settle you into the present moment.

If you want to feel calm, breathe calm. If you want to feel peaceful, breathe peacefully. Breathe freely and you will slow down the crazy. If your goal while living this busy life of caring for others is to be unrushed, clear minded, and full of positive energy, intentionally breathe in a slow, deliberate, even-keeled fashion. Pausing to refuel with your breath can halt you from saying something you don't want to say and from doing something you don't want to do.

My anxiety attacks taught me it wasn't the paper bag that got me breathing normally again—it was awareness of my breath. **Choosing to tap into my breath is the fuel that brings me home to myself.** This gives me freedom and hope.

I invite you to become aware the next time you're not in the present moment and use **your inhale and exhale to bring you back to now.** Everyone will reap the benefit.

REFILL REFLECTION:

- Don't wait until an anxiety or panic attack to open your gift—your breath.
- For starters, schedule a time once a day to be with your breath for thirty seconds.
  - Thirty seconds; you can do anything for thirty seconds.
  - Increase time to one minute when you're ready for more.
  - When once a day is working well, increase frequency.
  - Find the duration and frequency that works for you.
  - If thirty seconds once a day is all you have the space for, perfect—that short amount of time is fuel that counts.
- Fill your Cup.

SIP 3.

THE FOUR REFILLS

——

You have four ways to get present and these are the four different approaches to filling your Cup: physically, mentally, emotionally, or spiritually.

Four women walk into a bar. They are all one refill away from holding a full Cup. The first woman needs a nap. The second needs time alone with a good book. The third woman is exactly where she needs to be, laughing with her three best friends. The fourth woman will be completely connected, aligned, and at peace when she can have a walk in the forest tomorrow morning.

We have more than one way to refill our souls with nourishing, life-giving fuel. Some days you need to move your body and others to rest or inspire it. There are different ways of connecting to yourself, and not only do your needs change, but you also change. I invite you to recognize your present needs on a moment-to-moment, day-to-day basis and leave the past and the future in their place. As you learn the different ways to fuel up and recalibrate, pay attention to what fits for you now, not for the you of last month, year, or decade. The present version of you invites you to **be here now**.

PHYSICAL REFILL:
- This is about your physical environment and your physical body.
- Check the space you are in; what needs to shift?
- Tune in to your body.
    - This is about moving your body in ways that feel good and empowering.
    - Rest your body and listen to it.
    - Feed your body with foods and beverages that bring out your healthiest, strongest self and feel good going in (and out).

Refill Ideas: Playing, exercising, eating, and moving your body in ways that **feel nourishing**. Rearranging or organizing your space, sage, feng shui, painting a room, getting a massage, visiting a naturopath or acupuncturist, going for a bike ride, a few stretches or three favorite yoga poses, dancing in the kitchen, signing up for a marathon and training for it, making yourself lunch and sitting down to eat it, drinking enough water, or putting up your feet to rest.

MENTAL REFILL:
- Challenge, entertain, grow, or rest your mind.
- Spend time using your brain in ways that inspire and motivate.
- What you think matters: Choose your thoughts about yourself and others wisely.

- Get in the habit of using mantras, affirmations, and words that support your growth and inspire your mind. The recording in your head that you listen to about yourself, minute after minute and day after day, must be one that lifts you up.

Refill Ideas: Writing, reading, meditating, a crossword puzzle, cooking, planning, building, designing, organizing, creating, coloring, and resting your mind—unplug from technology and thinking. Have a basket filled with books and materials that **mentally stimulate and inspire** you, and keep this basket organized and easily accessible. Limit time on your phone to activities and scrolling that supports and motivates. Participate in groups that ignite enthusiasm and food for thought. Start your day with positive intention and create time to speak out or write mantras and affirmations that promote possibility daily. Even short moments of rest and quiet throughout the day clears your head and diminishes stress.

EMOTIONAL REFILL:

- Honor, express, and listen to your emotions.
- You're not your emotions; however, they show up to be your teacher, to guide, and to invite you to pay attention. Emotions are your thermometer as you take your temperature to understand what needs recognizing, honoring, and expressing in the moment.
- You experience hundreds of emotions in any given day, and when the big ones are ignored, they will continue to come back for a visit until you pay attention and express them in a healthy, helpful way.

- Emotions like anger are not "bad," and they need a proper vehicle of expression.
- Emotions are a road map guiding you to where you need to go next.

Refill Ideas: Connect with those people with whom you can safely express your emotions, watch a movie and laugh or cry your eyes out, check in with yourself periodically throughout the day to notice your emotional temperature, engage with others regularly **where your feelings are honored**—dinners out with friends, phone calls, and texting communication—listen to music, journal, and in person interactions that feed your emotions positively.

SPIRITUAL REFILL:

- No matter your beliefs, you're a spiritual being who requires connection.
- An energy that is larger than your soul pulsates, vibrates, and lives all around you. When your soul connects to that life force, the divinity within you ignites.
- Within the trees, ocean, air, the person in front of you, and within you there is love, holy energy, and life—it is up to you to tap into that power, grace, and strength.
- This type of refill is personal. Your relationship with Spirit is a relationship only you can define. No religion or person holds the key. This relationship is yours and yours alone to unlock.

Refill Ideas: Get out into nature, pray alone or with another regularly, meditate, light a candle, create a sacred altar in your home, attend a church service, sing, dance, participate in rituals that feed your spirituality, read poetry or theology, ignite your spiritual relationship by listening to the still small voice within, and celebrate love and life in all its forms. **Find your own version of church,** whether that is in a church every Sunday, with your yoga community every Saturday, or every night around the dinner table with those you love. Welcome Grace in all you do. Ask for help and expect it. Have faith in receiving help and accept it when it comes from another person, for that is Spirit in the face of another.

For all the refills above, *please*:

- Replace *should* with *must.*
- Drop comparison to others and versions of self from the past. I repeat, no comparison allowed. You needed one particular fuel yesterday, but today is a new day.

Whether you require a refill to adjust your environment, listen to your body, learn something new, have a belly laugh with a friend, a good cry alone, or commune with your version of God in a field or in a church, get really good at noticing what is missing and honoring that absence by pouring it for yourself. You're the only one who knows what you need, and you're the only one who can pull up to the refill tank and receive. As you honor the different ways to refill, **leave comparison at the back door.**

REFILL REFLECTION:

- Get clear each morning about at least one of the four refills you will honor that day.
- Check in and ask yourself which refill is needed.

- For each of the four refill categories, have a ready idea of ways you like to refill and you know work for you.
- Don't make this process complicated; at least one thing to honor at least one refill method.
- Fill your Cup.

SIP 4.

LISTEN TO THE NUDGE

---

*That whisper calling your
name holds the answers.*

One morning more than seven years ago, while minding my own business, I received the nudge to text my niece Katherine. She had recently given birth to her first child and happened to live down the street from me, and I had been giving her little family space. I was about to go on a walk when I received the poke to invite her and her newborn daughter. Katherine is not one to have her phone nearby, nor does she check it often.

Reach out, the nudge came again when my head tried to analyze and talk myself out of reaching out to Katherine. I was confident in the decision to text her despite it not sounding logical. The gentle, repetitive nudge was a loud interruption to my thoughts and schedule. I listened to the voice, knowing it had supported me in the past. Within fifteen minutes, we were on a walk together.

Divine timing? A coincidence? A voice. A whisper. An idea out of the blue. A repeated prodding, a continual poke. All nudges from your wise self, Spirit, Universe, or your Aunt Betty. All trustworthy and reliable. (I don't have an Aunt Betty, but my deceased grandmother is constantly trying to get my attention. That, too, is a Divine nudge.)

Whomever the source, something or someone is trying to get our attention.

Have you had the stars align for you like this? Putting typical routine, experience, and logic aside, were you surprised by the gift of the nudge? The longer you put off responding to these pokes, the more times you will be prodded, which can be reassuring or a pain in the ass. **The nudge is not only an idea. It's an invitation.** You always get the choice to respond to it or not. The more you learn to get out of your head and drop down into your body and receive the message, the more it will happen. If you are used to sticking to the plan, deciding everything with that beautiful mind of yours, it may sound strange, unorthodox, or even ridiculous. I encourage you to lean in and listen to the ridiculous.

Call this person; reach out and ask them; turn left instead of right; do this differently; walk down this aisle even though you normally avoid it, all nudges.

Walking with my niece that morning, we both honored more whispers that came our way. Our conversation turned toward childcare and returning to work. One new thought after another sparked me sharing a nanny lead, another out of the blue nudge that led to my niece finding a nanny who, more than seven years later, is still the nanny to now both of her children.

This reminds me of the nudge I shared with you in the "Introduction" about writing this book. At the time, I had absolutely no idea what the whisper fully meant, *Write a book and call it* Mama Needs a Refill.

I was clueless of all the steps that would follow. Some nudges are for the moment, small pokes guiding you, and other times, the nudges may reveal their potency and importance in the distant future.

Start a meditation practice. Read that book. Learn that language. Stop and say hi to your neighbor. Whispers that may lead to a new teacher, a friend lending you a book, a trip of a lifetime, helping out a neighbor in need, or discovering your fuel.

When I started writing this book fourteen years ago, I called the nudge God. Some days I call the nudge my wise self and other days my Cup. You get to call your nudge what you want. Whether it's your soul getting your attention or Divine Energy lining up to support you. Call it Joe. Regardless of your belief system that taps on your shoulder, there are no accidents. Notice the gentle whispers, poke in the gut, physical sensation—all signaling you to pay attention and listen up. All guideposts encouraging you along the path to your goals, dreams, and vision.

You are invited to pay attention; answer the summons. Be willing to get out of your head, step off your beaten path, and listen to the voice calling your name. This voice is full of love, positivity, and possibility.

REFILL REFLECTION:

- The next time you get a nudge and you can't physically attend to it in the moment, write it down.
- Start a nudge notebook.
  - Keep your notebook accessible in your car, purse, or kitchen counter, preferably wherever you get most of your nudges.
- Interview your nudge with provoking questions:
  - What do you want me to know?
  - Do you really want me to do that?
  - What is stopping me?
- Your soul needs you to move your feet and do the work.
- Fill your Cup.

TAP IN

———

*You have a well of answers within
you ready to give you direction, point
the way, and lead you home.*

"I want to do what God wants me to do."

I said this in my first session with Julie, my spiritual director—a life coach for your spiritual relationship. We met in her office twice, and now many years later, her words still provide a great balm for my spirit.

"And what do you think God wants you to do?"

My intention for meeting Julie was to figure out my life, as I had come to a crossroads and was struggling to figure out my path and my next direction. I didn't know which course or turn to take. I was overwhelmed and confused by my choices.

Have you ever been at a crossroads wondering what in the hell you're supposed to do with your life? If you have little ones at home, raising them doesn't always feel rewarding or purposeful, and even in that busy time, there are moments of **wondering what you're supposed to be doing with your life**. As if raising a family isn't enough, we yearn for more. If your children are grown and out of the house, it may be time for a whole new direction. Your current job may be making you annoyed and unhappy. These are normal intersections in life, piecing together our desires, needs, longings, and purpose and turning them into some sort of plan. It seems to me every time my kids are going through a new phase, I am there next to them, ready to find a new route myself. As this book releases, our youngest will be starting college. Life can be an extended and continuous invitation to curiosity. *What now? What next? How? When?*

Your inner wisdom is ready to guide you. She will poke you when you're not paying attention and speak to you when you ask for guidance. This inner wisdom answers your questions with all the answers that **already exist inside of you**. In the previous "Sip," we learned about the nudge and how it can show up. As you practice listening to the nudge, you will befriend your inner wisdom and strengthen the connection between the two. We all possess insight and clarity that is ready to provide answers to our questions and guide us on our path. You don't need to acquire a special degree, password, or endorsement of any kind to unleash this bank of knowledge. The only requirement is that you ask the question for which you are seeking guidance and **listen for the answer**.

When I sought out Julie's help, I wanted her to tell me which way to turn and what to focus on next. I was ready for the next chapter and overwhelmed with which page to turn. I paused for a long time when she asked me what I believed God wanted me to do. Then the answer came to me. I could barely get out the words, choking through my tears.

"God probably wants me to be happy and do what I want to do."

Bingo.

This goes back to the introduction of our Cup and Spirit being a united force. My will and Divine will are the same. You, too, have a Divine knowing within. Tap into your agency and become clear with where you want to turn next. Your highest self knows. It's like having your own compass in your back pocket.

Asking for guidance, tuning in to the answers offered, and observing and acting on what you hear all get **easier with practice**. You might take some time to learn how your own guidance speaks to you as you become able to differentiate between fear and affirmation, worry and trust, but doing this is well worth the effort. Think of it as learning a new language, one of **faith over fear**. Once you're in the habit of doing this over and over again, you will learn to trust this guidance. Spirit has your back, and Spirit resides within. Your first step is to believe.

Believe in you. **Believe in the well of wisdom within.** Believe in the power of the Universe. You are not alone.

TAP IN:
- Start with the question that has you stuck.
- Ask it out loud.
- Listen for the answer.
- Keep asking; the answer will come when you're ready.
- If you're consistent with your question and no answer is coming, journal. Write the question with your dominant hand and answer with your nondominant hand.

- Get in the practice of listening to your body and spirit, not only your mind.

In "Sip 29," we will explore discernment in greater depth.

I believed my answers were out there somewhere rather than right inside of me. When I got in the habit of seeking my own counsel, I learned to trust my answers. The more questions I asked, the more nudges I received, and ultimately, the more guidance I was offered, affirming that my Cup was supporting me and leading the way.

Get in touch with your inner wisdom, your trusted compass. I invite you to become friends with your inner bank of knowledge and wisdom. Establishing this relationship may take practice, but once you confidently learn that your inner wisdom is there to support you, choosing your direction at a crossroads will become second nature.

REFILL REFLECTION:

- You have a knowing within that is waiting to be tapped into.
- The next time you come to a critical point or yearn for guidance, ask yourself, "What next? What do I do now?"
  - Then wait. Be still. Get out of your head and pay attention to the signs, the conversations going on around you, your physical cues, and your nudges.
  - The road signs are placed in your path—notice them.
- Practice patience and trust as you listen for the next guiding step.
- Fill your Cup.

SIP 6.

ROOTED

———

I stand up taller when I have taken
the time to connect to what matters
most, when I water my roots, and
when I place priority on my values.

In my early forties, I outgrew my relationship with my Higher Power. I still believed, only now with views of a God that were bigger than any theological definition or religion. My beliefs no longer fit one textbook description. I was thirsty for a deeper connection, more aligned with my truth that I wasn't finding in a church pew.

In *When the Heart Waits*, Sue Monk Kidd describes the chrysalis as her symbol of rebirth during her transformational process on her spiritual journey, also in her forties. Like the author discovering this symbol in a way she never expected, I, too, found my sign, my symbol, in my own backyard. During my transformational spiritual wake-up call, a.k.a. my midlife crisis minus the affair and convertible, trees became my sign. My symbol of Divine and Sacred Mystery.

Pruning our hydrangea one January, deep in contemplation about who God was to me and what I believed and no longer believed, I asked for a sign. A sign to show me the way, remind me I'm not alone, and direct me to know again that my life had purpose and meaning. While carrying a pile of branches to the yard waste bin, I looked up. I chose the tree as my **spiritual anchor**, my symbol of healing and growth. Or one could say the tree chose me. Perhaps an overly obvious choice as I live in the Northwest, where we have a plethora. Trees in all shapes, sizes, colors, and varieties adorn our street corners and backyards, line our highways, and cover the mountains. In my Seattle neighborhood, trees are everywhere. A particular Douglas fir growing in our backyard stopped me in my tracks, even though it had been there all along. Never mind, we had already been living there for over a decade.

Show me a sign.

In that same book, Kidd speaks of the chrysalis as the dark place where beauty can emerge. **A butterfly does not become a butterfly by skipping the cocoon period.**

The branches of the Douglas fir reached up to the sky as if to say, "I'm here. I'll show you the way."

I was invited to participate more fully in my life—the extension of branches of this particular tree called me in. I was reminded Spirit exists all around; I only need to notice. On my dog walks, I would ask a question, and the different trees in my neighborhood would answer. This became my **new way to pray**. Praying had always been a powerful and meaningful way for me to connect, and this new method of experiencing prayer on my daily walks became my new communion. Something new broke open within me. I received messages from the shape of the branches, form of the buds, and color of the leaves that only make sense to me.

"Relax and play more," one tree seemed to say, with the plastic red and yellow swing hanging from its sturdy branch.

"Stay aligned with your truth," urged a row of pear trees a few blocks down the street.

"Be patient," offered the newly budded tree that practically poked me on the head.

"Stop worrying."

"Stay grounded."

Simple suggestions that consoled my questioning mind and searching heart. The birch with its unique white trunk, her peeling bark posing like a scraped knee, is the tree that offers new beginnings. The fir tree in her year-round green dress offering honesty and truth, a pillar of strength for many people. The hemlock represents, on a spiritual level, protection for some and healing for others. I have heard others remark that the oak in all her beauty and glory represents strength and endurance.

I still embrace the basic tree, the one on the corner along my path, the one whose name I could not tell you, as my symbol of rebirth, growth, and transformation. My longing for a new connection and a more meaningful relationship with

God was delivered to me through something standing before me all along. A tower of strength continually offering me wisdom, awareness, and peace. Trees in all their shapes and sizes offer power and renewal, and I was ready to be rooted. I was awakened to being more than just a part of this world, but being one with Spirit.

A ballast to keep me from falling over, from drifting further away from myself. I would notice a tree when I was driving carpool, frustrated about a kid's meltdown, or feeling overwhelmed with all my responsibilities. My roots would find me again. **Faith was my number one root**—only now, it wasn't a religion that fed that faith—faith in something bigger than me, a belief, and trust without proof or biblical backup. An understanding without seeing. When my faith goes unwatered, not to be corny, I wilt.

Oh, yes. That's right. I'm not alone. I can do this. I can trust the unfurling, unfolding, and uncertainty.

Extended branches. The color green in all its shades. New buds. Holy Mystery. Spirit without a man-made religion or rules that confine, alienate, or ignore—all are welcome. A place to rest when weary. Shelter in the storm with a glance up to the moon or out to the ocean. Respite sitting under a tree in the yard. Reminders that meaningful connection is all around and doesn't have to wait until I walk into the doors of a sacred building.

Are you questioning your connection to something bigger than you? Are you looking for your own sign in the dark? Are you longing to be rooted?

Like any relationship, there are changes, and like any healthy relationship, there is questioning. When I hit my midlife moment of change and reconnection, I sought new definitions and found myself again. When my spiritual relationship turned stagnant, I **stepped out into nature** and became the crazy lady talking to the trees.

Has God been an integral part of your life, and now you're scratching your head a bit, ready for a reframe? Have you not let Spirit in because it was forced upon you, didn't align, and wasn't the right fit?

In times of curiosity and reflection, looking for information and inspiration in new places helps. For me, that meant turning to books and nature. Poets, mystics, teachers, and seekers all offering threads leading me to roots of connection, a foundation on which I could firmly stand. The first thing to do when on a spiritual quest is to be open. Pray in a way that makes sense to you, talk to those you trust, and look to the signs and symbols all around you.

Your spiritual connection is yours and yours alone. **I invite you to not take anyone else's definition as yours** and to be willing to grow, deepen, and strengthen this relationship if it calls you. What symbols are in front of you, wanting to help? Be curious. Allow yourself to think outside of the box. There very well may be something waiting to provide you clarity when you feel heavyhearted. A symbol or sign may be right in front of you as you seek comfort, guidance, support, and wisdom. Be open to receiving encouragement, inspiration, and direction from the thing standing in your yard or around the corner. A billboard, a bunny hopping along the side of the road, the light of the moon, or the shape of a cloud—all possible assistance. A word of strength, a sign of fertility, a new beginning, or your imagination—all offering ideas and help. Start asking your questions and **pay attention to the signs around you**.

Like a butterfly must live in the dark before growing wings, you too can benefit from your period of dormancy. What if you embraced the messy, dark, and tender parts? What if a new guide is waiting in your backyard to point the way home? I invite you to embrace a willingness to be open to discover new places that offer rich soil, looking at the signs in a different light. Periods of waiting can be where the true birthing and awakening take place in your soul. New places to grow deep meaningful roots.

REFILL REFLECTION:

- Give three minutes of your energy, attention, and time to yourself first thing in the morning.
- If you're holding your breath, know you're not alone.
- Figure out what your roots are and water them.
  - Mine are faith and connection. Discover yours and make them a priority.
- Release your breath and let the Universe catch it.
- If I had a prayer for you today, if you're dancing in the dark, it would be to not turn the page too quickly, for the reluctant darkness has its own whisper of light.
- Is there a symbol in nature that draws you in?
  - It's not a random thing that you love tulips, hummingbirds, or Japanese maples. These creations of nature may have a message, an inspiration, or a piece of wisdom to pass on.

- Do you see a repeated pattern of experiencing something in nature?
    - How can it offer solace?
    - How can it provide the answers for which you seek?
- Fill your Cup.

SIP 7.

BIRD CIRCLE

——

There is safety in a circle, all are included.
In a circle is where I find home.

"Mama, do you want to know what Mr. Chung does?"

My son was five and in the kitchen with me as I prepared dinner. Mr. Chung is a dinosaur bird character on the TV show *Dinosaur Train*.

"Please tell me."

"He does this," he sits cross-legged on the kitchen floor, hands resting on his knees, with his thumb and middle finger of each hand forming a circle.

"Aum."

Eyes closed, centered, and calm. I barely recognized my little boy.

Then, in a flash, his eyes open big and wide, he bounces to his feet and asks, "Can we have church after dinner?"

Ever since deciding to leave the disconnected experience of Catholic mass in exchange for family circle, we gathered in the living room to light a candle on the coffee table. Daughter played a song on the piano or read us a poem. Son chose one of his stuffed animals, and we used it as a talking piece. As we passed the stuffed monkey, we took turns sharing our gratitude or anything else we wanted to talk about.

"I'm thankful for my family and this roof over our heads."

Our son passes the stuffed animal to his sister, who decides to pass, keeping her prayers and words close to her heart.

It's all good. No rules here at "family church" except to listen and respect each other as we take turns sharing. Communion, my favorite part of church, doesn't need the blessing of a priest. We have each other. Chocolate or Goldfish are great substitutes for the Communion Host. (Tastes a lot better too.)

"You are whole, Daddy, and I love you as you are. May this bless you."

With tears in his eyes, it's my husband's turn. Not a man who grew up Catholic, he picked up his cue and created his own blessing to our daughter.

"May you know you're loved, beautiful girl."

My daughter lets the chocolate melt in her mouth as she turns to me, now a blubbering mess of love and tears, "Mama, this is the body of Christ."

Nothing says holy, Christ, unity, and love more than connection with my family. I don't need to be in a church building receiving a wafer from an ordained person. I'm home. I'm in Heaven, right here.

I love that sitting in a yoga position like Mr. Chung the dinosaur bird makes my son think of church. What makes you think of church? Where do you feel connected to others or Spirit? Where do you feel at home?

Church isn't only a place you visit. It's **a place you create**. A place to build, nurture, grow, and evolve your spiritual connection. When was the last time you experienced church?

I have clients who experience church every Saturday during the winter ski season in the mountains, every night around the dinner table with their family, on their daily morning walk with their best friend, or at their yoga class in silence with strangers. Church is connection and fellowship, an honoring you get to define. If church is about growing in faith and relationship, it must leave you a little different—cracked wide open for more love and light to get in and bless you. For in that Divine connection, when your best self is recharged, you take that blessing and shine it out to others.

I came to this definition hearing firsthand from clients the disconnection they experienced in a church pew, hall, or temple and from my own personal experience of leaving

Sunday Mass empty. Rather than racing out the door each week, leaving Dad, who didn't attend mass with us, at home, we chose to try something new. This practice of home church became our **circle of love, fostering connection** with each other as well as our own individual relationships with Spirit.

This breaking bread and sharing communion as a family is the nugget that fed me spiritually when we stopped going to Catholic Mass. In our intentional gathering is where I feel vulnerable, blessed, and connected. In relationship with my husband, daughter, and son is where I experience Christ's love and fellowship. Sharing in gratitude, prayer, and blessing, I see the face of God in those faces in our living room. There may be another season where I find and attend an actual building that is called a church to receive spiritual nourishment. These days it is over dinner with my family, praying with a neighbor, walking in the woods, or seated around the table with friends that **I experience church in the greatest sense**. A sacred connection, a holy experience that unites me with Spirit as I leave a little bit different, a bit more whole.

YOU GET TO CREATE CHURCH. CHOOSE WHAT FEEDS YOU.

There are many ways to experience church, in the old-fashioned sense of the word. If experiencing church is an important value for you now in your life, you get to define it and create it on your terms. Honor what is important to you now, not ten years ago. Pay attention to the experience you are desiring versus the one you are experiencing. You get to create something new.

REFILL REFLECTION:

- Is church important to you?
  - Establish what qualities and values of church are important.
- Are you actively attending or creating church that refills and recharges, blesses, and grows your own personal connection to Spirit or your Cup?
- Notice where you feel light in your beliefs and ideas around church.
- Let go of should. No loving Spirit points fingers, and no one can tell you where and when you feel most connected.
- Dance in the mystery of discovering and creating your church of choice.
- Fill your Cup.

SIP 8.

BE. HERE. NOW.

———

The present moment is all we have.

"Can I ask you something?"

"Let me finish what I'm doing so I can listen with my full attention."

"Oh, sure, Mom."

This is *not* how it used to go in our house. Getting here took practice. I would be in the kitchen cooking dinner, emotionally fried, scrolling mindlessly on my phone. A call from a family member or someone coming into the kitchen was an invasion of my privacy. When I had an empty Cup, I didn't respond with kindness.

"Now what?"

One evening, in particular, we got home late from soccer practice. Everyone was hungry, one kid had a bad day and wanted to tell me about it, the dog needed to be let outside, and I was exhausted. I put dinner in the oven and checked my phone. Busy being the cook, the driver, the counselor, and the candlestick maker for everyone but myself landed me on my phone scrolling mindlessly. Not even hungry for food, I stuffed a handful of chips in my mouth and considered bingeing a Netflix show. Fully absorbed in others' social media feeds, unaware of the dog scratching at the back door and a kid standing next to me wanting a hug.

The fire alarm goes off; dinner is burned.

Carol Anne Gotbaum is one of my inspirations for this book. Her story is of a woman realizing she needs support with her alcohol addiction. I read about this affluent, well-educated, beautiful, intelligent woman who married into a prominent family in *People* magazine at my acupuncturist's office.

On her way to rehabilitation, Carol decided to have one last drink in the airport. That drink turned into more than one and was combined with prescription medication, which caused her to be wildly frustrated when she discovered her flight was overbooked. That episode landed her in an airport jail. When she was arrested by airport police, her now-public recorded last words were, "I am not a terrorist. I am a sick mom. I need help" (Ravitch 2011).

Her story spoke to me on many levels. I am not an alcoholic and don't struggle with life-altering addiction or depression, but I have been so low that, in my imagination, I wanted out of my life. As Carol's story goes, she accidentally strangled herself trying to free herself of handcuffs. No one came to her aid, and she died in an airport jail. She sought support, I imagine because she loved her children and recognized she couldn't do it alone.

This is where I invite you to seek professional help if addiction or depression have you confined to your own prison. Therapy is life-changing; seeking help and recognizing support is life-giving. I'm a mom who has been lost. I am a person who has reached out for help, and it didn't cost me my life like it did Carol. Different than the tragic cases of mom's falling into a deep depression and suffering from addiction, and not to dilute its devastating outcome, we all have our breaking point. If depression and addiction are part of your story, you are not alone, and I invite you to put down this book and seek professional support now. **Moving forward is a courageous act** when it requires looking at your past. You are worth making that step.

This brings me back to where we started. If you aren't taking care of what you need now and are shoving down your feelings, distracting yourself with your phone, TV, food, or any other drug of choice, you aren't the only one feeling the effects.

The **biggest Cup drainer of them all is not being in the present moment**. When your thoughts are on how you should've worded that email or on the call you need to make, everyone in front of you feels it. If your child wants to tell you about a class assignment, or your business partner wants to explain a report, and your thoughts and energy are focused elsewhere, everyone feels your distraction. Even if you appear to be listening, they know you aren't. Your tone and body language say it all.

When you notice you're not present, call a do-over. Let the person in front of you know you have a lot on your mind, and you need one minute to switch gears to get present, to hear all about what they want to tell you. Be transparent with your spouse, friend, colleague, or child that you need a second to step into this moment.

Kids appreciate authenticity—everyone does. Be transparent. When you speak out about where you need to make an adjustment, your child will remember that and know they can come to you with news they want to share. This **builds trust for the future**. When they come to you about the big stuff on their mind, they will have an unconscious memory that you are a good listener. Be the model of practicing presence; it will teach them to do the same in this busy world of distraction.

"Do I have your full attention?"

"Do you need a minute to get present?"

A question. A pause. A minute to shift **creates a wake-up call to the present moment**. Being patient, genuine, kind, and compassionate is impossible when you don't even hear what the person in front of you is saying. All that matters in that moment is the person standing next to you in the kitchen. The email or dinner can wait. (Please turn off the burner.)

Getting present removes a huge battle. When you practice being present the overwhelm vanishes, and any friction and confusion disappear. I promise I'm not yanking your chain on this: The more you **practice engagement in the present moment, the more of an active participant in life you**

become. The more fully alive and awake you are to yourself, the more present you are to your children, partner, and to all those involved. As you tune in to the person or experience right in front of you, put down your phone, turn off the noise in your head, separate from the distraction, and come down to planet Earth, **the fuller your Cup will be**.

If you are a mom, you may be thinking you're the one who is responsible for everything. Therefore, it is impossible to avoid thinking about the future, as who else will think about washing the soccer uniform or buying the gift for the party? That's where you can write things down. Your list will help you keep track. For now, be with the one telling you the story, standing with you in the kitchen. Tomorrow they will be off to college, and the day after that they'll be making dinner for their own children. The past is gone, and the future comes fast enough.

Be. Here. Now. The present is a beautiful gift to open.

When you are being present not only to the people in front of you but also to the task before you, your energy will not be depleted as quickly. When you pay attention to the email you're writing, the dinner you're cooking, or the conversation you're having, the more focused and productive you become. If you run into someone you didn't want to see and you allow the interaction to unfold, you'll also notice that by giving up control and being present the unexpected conversation flows. When you **lean into the flow** instead of fighting it, the experience turns out to be exactly what you needed as the conversation offers a lesson or a nugget of reflection that later leads to your awareness and growth.

REFILL REFLECTION:

- The next time you catch yourself only being physically present and mentally on another planet, stop.
- What is it you need to do to focus your attention, mind, and awareness on the present moment?
- What is your relationship to addiction and depression?
- Is it time to take that courageous step and receive support?
- Give yourself time, space, and attention to adjust to the present moment.
  - A day can hold so much.
  - A moment can only hold one thing.
  - Allow yourself the time to find your breath and focus on what is here and now.
- Fill your Cup.

SIP 9.

ONE CANDLE

———

Rituals are the formulas by
which harmony is restored.
—TERRY TEMPEST WILLIAMS

"Pray for my mom. She has surgery tomorrow."

I hang up the phone with my friend and light a candle. My wordless prayer becomes a ritual of love.

The difference between a ritual and a routine is that a **ritual provides connection, pause, reflection, and meaning to something within your soul**. A routine is an automatic consistent action, like brushing your teeth before washing your face. As much as brushing your teeth is a necessary part of your bedtime routine, it doesn't serve as a bridge from your soul to Spirit. Possibly you are not looking to walk any bridge from your soul to Spirit. You simply want to be clean before bed. (Often a good plan.) For me, if I haven't experienced a meaningful connection, I hit the pillow at night empty and depleted. A ritual infuses meaning behind the action and adds fulfilling connection to my daily tasks. If you think of three people you love while brushing your teeth and give thanks for them being in your life, that is a ritual. I even call it a prayer. A ritual can open your mind to a deeper connection with Spirit or your soul and provide strength and grounding.

I would guess you have seasonal rituals. Cue the Christmas music, Hanukkah festivities, or Halloween jack-o'-lanterns. Beyond special occasions, I have daily rituals that create personal meaning, as filling my spiritual Cup is what matters most to me. I'm all about purposeful connection, whether it's to my best self, Spirit, or another person.

I invite you to think about the rituals you once participated in that meant a lot to you as well as the ones you actively honor or are curious about bringing into your life. A lot of my rituals stem from over forty years of being a practicing Catholic. Even though I am no longer participating in that religion, some rituals are ingrained deeply. The sign of the cross at the end of our mealtime prayer or when an ambulance passes unites me to the moment. No longer connecting me to the religion but joining me with Spirit and my Cup.

Although my intention is to get you thinking about daily rituals that can align, support, and guide you, I encourage you to be cognizant of the seasonal rituals you partake in. Some basic guidelines may be helpful for your seasonal traditions:

- Am I doing this because it feeds me or because everyone is expecting me to do it?
- After participation, is my Cup empty or full?
- Is it time to skip this practice and start something meaningful in its place?

I skip rituals to prevent burnout, and I decide that season if I have the bandwidth for it. I send out Christmas cards every other year, ask for help from family with the traditions that require a lot of time and effort, and say **no to any engagement if the stress is greater than the joy of participation.**

Let's explore daily ritual possibilities. A ritual can be meaningful and short at the same time. Here are some ideas to get you inspired into action:

POSSIBLE DAILY RITUALS:
- Pull a card from an oracle or inspirational deck.
- Write down three things you appreciate in a gratitude journal.
- Text a friend with daily gratitude.
- Step outside and speak your thanks and appreciation to the trees and sky.
- Write or speak out your daily intention. "Today I will practice presence."
- Have an altar in your home with objects that invoke meaning and stand in front of it for a few minutes, asking for guidance, giving thanks, and listening for wisdom.
- Sit drinking your favorite hot beverage until it is finished, with your phone turned off, listening to the stillness.
- Say a prayer, sing a prayer, or dance a prayer.
- Before your run or workout, do one yoga pose before you stretch.
- Use crystals, essential oils, or Reiki for purification and grounding.
- Write or speak affirmations. "I am strong."

- Sit with a pet and together breathe in the silence and sacredness of the moment.
- Three inhales and exhales.

You can incorporate rituals into your daily routine and responsibilities. Sing while doing the dishes or shaving your legs. Think of everyone and everything for which you are grateful as you make your bed. Light a candle at mealtime. The simplest action can deepen the everyday mundane activities, helping you to live intentionally. That is indeed the power of ritual—to bless all you do at a deeper level, beyond the action itself (Drucker 2018). As you practice your ritual, hold the bigger picture in mind: to be connected, to align with your best self, to honor life, or to become centered and grounded. Ultimately, when there is meaning and fulfillment, there is a greater opportunity to be holding a full Cup. Honor the longings of your soul.

REFILL REFLECTION:

- What daily ritual do you currently practice that could use an update or change so it continues to feed you and you actually show up regularly to honor it?
- Pick something from the list above and try it for two weeks.
- Notice how you can breathe blessing, gratitude, and intention into your daily activities and responsibilities.
- Fill your Cup.

SIP 10.

COMMIT

—

There comes a time when excuses get really boring and no longer work at convincing yourself to not do what you know you must.

Think of all the times you've put off the thing you really, really want to do. You sign up for a class, activity, project, or great idea and don't follow through because you have too much on your plate already or you signed up for the wrong reasons. The excuses will always be there when something feeds you physically, mentally, emotionally, or spiritually and especially when it checks off all four ways to refill. The excuses must be ignored. Are you ready to show up and be committed?

What is your current physical refill that is actually a refill on many levels as it feeds your mind and nourishes your Spirit? Bikram yoga was that for me; it checked off all four refill boxes—it was sex, a dopamine hit, meditation, and church all in one. I got sweaty, saw angels, emerged with a smile on my face, and gained muscles I never knew existed.

This commitment cured ailments and brought me to self-compassion. What was even more Cup filling was that I became a nice mom again, not yelling nearly as much, and I'm pretty sure I didn't swear nearly as often during those seven years of Bikram when our kiddos were little. (Don't quote me on the swearing part.)

I thought about this commitment for a couple of years before I signed up. The classes were expensive and took up a lot of time for a mom with young ones at home. But Bikram was the hallelujah to my longing for stillness, the catalyst for building muscle, and such a sanity saver. The release of tension in my body created space in my heart to approach parenting and life with more spaciousness; the focused devotion to showing up to something that was all for me benefited the entire family.

What is it for you? What's going to be your **saving grace** during this season you are in?

Seasons change. I was a runner before having kids and a Bikram yoga practitioner when my kids were in grade school. I found rowing when my children were in high school, and walking has been part of all my seasons, especially when we had a dog. What season are you in? This means what is calling you and what do you have the time and energy for.

The steps to making a commitment are as follows: **awareness, mindset, intention, and accountability**. Get clear on the promise you want to make to yourself. Let's break down the steps below.

SHOW UP AND COMMIT TO SELF:

Awareness provides the clear path toward making any commitment stick. Notice your interests. Pay attention to the ones you know you have the energy to carry out. Other things may be interesting, inviting for certain, but if you get honest with yourself, you're not truly devoted if your commitment stops with your enthusiasm. I can get super excited about learning how to paint and that is where my commitment currently starts and stops. As nice as it would be to have the natural ability to sit down in front of a blank canvas and fill it, I know I'm not 100 percent excited or devoted to this right now in my life. **When your heart is not fully invested, you are likely to not take your idea very far.** What do you wake up thinking about? Is a particular idea haunting you, in a good way, every night before you fall asleep? Pay attention to what you're talking about yet not showing up for. These thoughts are signaling that your path is opening up.

It's all about your **mindset**. This is an opportunity to take a real hard look at your readiness to not let anything prevent you from getting started. **Your attitude must match your readiness to not let anything stand in your way.** The specifics of circumstance need not matter when you have a positive, open, willing, "let's do this" attitude. Be willing to take a good look at your readiness to overcome any obstacle that appears on your path. *Can I do this? Do I want to do this?* What disturbance or minor irritant can you set aside? What is greater, the value the commitment fulfills or the drawback of any annoyance or inconvenience it may cause? You can only fake yourself out for so long when it comes to showing up to something in your life. Eventually, small frustrations will win out if you are not completely attached to making it work.

The third step requires 100 percent pure **intention**. You have this goal, this thing you're about to execute with your body, mind, and soul. What exactly is your intention behind it all? Get clear with the motivation behind the action. Does the thing you want to commit to genuinely fit your intention? Does your intention match your true desire? For example, let's say you want to take up yoga for the sole purpose of becoming more present, calm, and peaceful in your day-to-day life, and on your way to and from yoga you are screaming for everyone to get out of your way, running over small children, and biting off everyone's head before, during, and after class. If the class changes this behavior over time, you have an aligned match. Make a choice that matches your intention.

For some reason, we show up for others more readily than we do for ourselves. This is where **accountability** comes into play. To be accountable means to do what you say you will do. Essentially, accountability is about showing up to yourself. Once you're clear on your new chosen commitment that supports your values and you're in an activated mindset, it's time to make it real. **Find the frequency that works for you, releasing other people's assertions and agenda.** You may choose something you want to do once a month—twelve times a year may be all you need. If that thing is reading one book, you will have read twelve books in one year when you haven't finished a book since college. Choose your number wisely, as it only has to make sense to you. If after choosing your number and going forth with your commitment you pause to evaluate and notice you're not honoring your pledge, strongly consider the benefit of the incentive. Would you show up to yourself knowing you had to report your progress to another person? Knowing you get to share your development with someone who is rooting for you to succeed can be a substantial reason to get the ball rolling. **Writing your commitment down and speaking it out are two proven successful methods of seeing a commitment to completion.** Get your chosen commitment on the calendar, show up, and then celebrate your victory.

REFILL REFLECTION:

- Plug in to your **awareness.**
- Develop a healthy **mindset.**
- Set your **intention** wisely.
- Be **accountable.**
- Cease talking about your intention; choose to commit.
  - Choose the number of times in a day, week, month, or year you want to participate in this activity. Play around until you find your own magic number.
  - Write this activity down on your calendar.
  - Tell others.
  - Schedule your commitment like you would a child's dentist appointment or a lunch date with Oprah.
  - Show up and act as if it matters to you.
- Fill your Cup.

SIP 11.

HOLDING UP A MIRROR

———

Judgment aimed at others is really about us.

That hedge over there would look better if it was trimmed and reshaped. That yard needs weeding. That porch pot could use some love.

On a walk, a number of years ago, one spring morning, this was the conversation I was having with myself. Of all things, I was judging the landscapes in people's yards. Weird judgments on plants. I noticed this was something I often did. I looked at things with judgment, wanting to fix and change them, to make them better. That morning's observation went deep quickly as I realized I did the same thing with people, constantly having an inner dialogue of judging them and sizing them up.

She's too much. She's too nice. She's so this or way too much that.

Wow. I was not sure why I had turned into Judge Judy. This awareness nearly stopped me in my tracks. Behind this judgment of others, **I was really disapproving of myself.** Pointing the finger at others is only what appears on the surface, when in truth, I am demonstrating dissatisfaction with myself.

I'm too nice. I say too much. I say too little.

My judgments of plants and people and everything else in between stemmed from **not accepting myself, from not loving me as is.** This started when I was a young girl, somewhere around the age of nine, thinking I failed by not saving my parents' marriage. I unconsciously beat myself up, turning the judgment on myself. *Be better, so you aren't left. Smile wider, so you'll be accepted.* I believe all this internal criticism was birthed out of not having my mom around, having my father removed from our house, and feeling afraid of being abandoned. **Emotional abandonment can lead to unconscious wounds.** I was protecting myself in a weird, unsupportive way. *I don't want to be left again or hurt again. I will find a reason to not accept myself.*

The first day of Lent had arrived. That season of reflection and preparation that runs forty days until Easter. For those of you not familiar, Lent is the time of year Catholics give up something: TV, candy, sugar, alcohol, meat, eating between meals, and more. In the past I, too, tried my efforts of giving things up. Three years in a row I gave up swearing. Shit, shit, shit. You can guess how that turned out. I gave up meat, sugar, alcohol, and mayonnaise, my personal vice, but deprivation never brought me closer to God. These things never made me an instrument of peace, but rather they left me frustrated and feeling like a failure. My reasons were always self-focused, *I can lose weight during Lent if I give up 'sinful' foods.*

Years before that particular Lent, instead of focusing on "giving up" something, I looked at the season as a time to "take on" something. To "be" the change I desired. I took on meditating ten minutes every day, sitting in silence, and saying something kind to others. These efforts brought me a lot closer to anything Divine than "giving up" ever had.

That Lenten season, I chose to take the Catholic approach. I chose to give up something. I chose something that gets in the way of me living fully far more than a glass of wine, tacos, or a chocolate chip cookie, and trust me, it was a lot more challenging.

I gave up judgment. The time had come to release the hold this self-criticism had on me. Giving up judgment wasn't easy at first as I noticed how much it occupied my mind. As I noticed "things" in others that could be "better," I flipped the scenario over to me and asked what I was judging in myself. The next step was to **practice self-love and acceptance.** With many attempts of stumbling and trying again, I learned how to release my critical self-talk.

RELEASE CRITICAL SELF-TALK:
- Catch yourself in the act.
  - Notice the tone, words, attitude, and message you are telling yourself.
- Forgive yourself for talking that way.
- Be curious about where this self-talk is coming from.
- Start over: Choose another tone, words, attitude, and message to tell yourself.

Once I did this, I noticed the whole person in front of me without an agenda of how to change or fix them from head to toe. **Judgment of others, which is really judgment of myself, stands in the way of loving fully and unconditionally.** I no longer saw people as needing to be changed but as perfect and whole beings. That Lenten season had a powerful result as my release of judgment spilled over to the next season and the next, until judgment was no longer a major part of me.

This is now a new part of my being. I am lighter for not carrying the heavy burden of judgment. Others never needed to change; my self-acceptance needed to be turned on its head. When you have self-acceptance, acceptance of others follows suit. When you're hurt by others' spoken or assumed judgments of you, will you recognize it is about them and not you? When you're judging others, will you go within and recognize what is really going on?

REFILL REFLECTION:

- Is there something you want to give up or take on that can lead you to live life more fully?
- How is judgment of others a reflection on you?
- How is judgment keeping you separated from others or yourself?
- Fill your Cup.

SIP 12.

CHOOSE JOY

—

Find out where joy resides and give
it a voice far beyond singing. For
to miss the joy is to miss all.

—ROBERT LOUIS STEVENSON

"Come up; you must be Jenny."

I made an appointment with a massage therapist whom I
heard had the gift of connecting with the deceased loved
ones of the client she was working on. The day I met Beth
was bright and sunny, and her warm welcome matched the
weather. The yard leading up to the porch was ordained with
meticulously pruned shrubs. A gurgling fountain and a god-
dess statue nestled under a tree caught my attention on my
way to the stairs. Bamboo towered over a bench. I was drawn
in by the simple, Zen-like oasis that felt part English cottage,
part Japanese monastery.

Not only was I seeking relief from back, hip, and neck pain,
but I was also mentally stuck. I had been pondering a career

move. I was exhausted from the stage both of my children were in, and I was longing for something new, different, and meaningful in my life. My body carried all this. I didn't have to speak out my pain as Beth ushered me up the stairs. We sat on the porch swing, discussing my aches and pains and getting clear on what I was hoping to release. I didn't mention my longing or my being mentally and emotionally stuck. I had no words for my overwhelm.

She led me into a beautiful room decorated with Buddha and Kuan Yin statues, a painting of Ganesh, and bamboo shoji screens. Undressing alone, I noticed how every piece of art in the room emitted beauty. I was already feeling tranquil. Our session began like any other massage I had experienced in the past. Her small hands were stronger than any person more than half her age. Beth was in her early seventies, and every wrinkle on her skin made her more beautiful. I was comfortable in her presence and easily melted into the massage table. She had been working on me for about twenty minutes when she let me know she was getting the sense that a presence and energy was with us.

"Do you know that sometimes your loved ones who have gone on to the next world stop by for a visit?"

She said this so calmly as if someone had forgotten their purse earlier and would be dropping by to retrieve it.

"Yes, that is one reason I am here."

Secretly hoping it was my father, who had died a few years earlier, I waited to hear what she had to say.

"Who do you know who died along with her two babies?"

"Marci," I told her.

I was stunned she was here. Marci lost her life while giving birth to twin boys in 1999. She was a new friend at the time of her death and the wife of our longtime friend Hayden.

"She wants you to know something."

Beth began to work on my feet, rubbing out the tendons and kneading my heels like pie dough.

"She says to find and do what brings you joy."

A smile crossed my face even though it was smooshed into the donut-shaped head pillow.

How did she know? Joy? Could this be the directional guidepost I was seeking?

I asked myself these questions. My body relaxed. Joy had been a teacher for me in the past. **Joy had helped me get unstuck before.** I had my head buried in the sand, focusing on raising our kids. I had forgotten to enjoy the process. When I am joyful, I am filled up. Even one spark of joy can carry through an entire day.

I could still talk through the hole, and I could see Beth's feet. The space between her big toes and second toes was more than an inch gap. I once read that the wider the space between those first toes, the more intuitive the person. Her toenails were painted bright red. How could you not love and trust this woman, part fairy godmother, part gypsy?

"I've been wrestling with what direction to go with my career while I have two young children at home. The message to do what brings me joy resonates."

"Someone else is here."

I was still expecting my dad.

"This woman is crying in a garden. She says to choose joy."

Dig up the joy, find it, and choose it, first from Marci and now from my maternal grandmother.

"Discover your joy."

Is this a message you need to hear right now, sitting on your own porch? For me, raising children wasn't always joyful. **Joy is a choice and looks different for everyone.** Joy can be experienced on a run, baking bread, volunteering, the moment each morning when you're alone with your cup of tea, or when you lift your babe out of the crib.

Joy is not necessarily something you see. It's something you feel. You feel joy in the tears running down your cheeks, the lightness in your heart, and the smile on your face. Joy can make the difference between wanting to stay in bed all day or to get up and participate in life. I needed a hall pass, a reminder that joy is not only something I value but also adds purpose and fulfillment.

Joy is waiting for you below the surface of what is challenging and hard in your life right now. Dig joy out, create it, discover it, and choose it. Notice what happens when you integrate joy into your life.

And whether or not you believe in the afterworld and guidance from loved ones who have gone before you, know you're not alone. Guidance and support are waiting all around you. Look up at the clouds, notice the stranger smiling, or see the art on the wall. Stick your head in the fountain and drink it up. Ask to be shown the way and follow the flower trail to your joy.

REFILL REFLECTION:

- When you find yourself a bit rudderless, find the joy.
- Then go out and do it.
    - Be it.
    - Create it.
    - Share it.
    - Receive it.
- Get out of your head and drop into your heart.
- Pull out your journal and answer the following:
    - What brings me joy?
    - What color is joy?
    - When was the last time I experienced joy?
    - What is one thing I can do every day that brings me joy?
- Fill your Cup.

ME, MYSELF, AND I

———

When I'm with me, myself, and I, we
know how to have a great time.

The text came after I was seated in the crowded restaurant.

"We are on our way, stuck in traffic, and won't arrive for another thirty minutes."

I had scrambled and hustled to meet Kristal and Angela at the restaurant on time, and now here I was, handed an unexpected gift. Thirty minutes is a lot of time to yourself when you've been with young kids all day and every minute of your day is planned.

"While you wait for your friends, can I get a drink started for you?"

"Yes, please."

As I was waiting for my dear friends to arrive, I slowly savored the most delicious margarita and pulled out the notebook

I carried in my purse. I wrote a poem. I doodled and day-dreamed on the blank page. Simple phrases strung together. An opportunity to be without an agenda.

Being alone brought back a time in my life when I was always eating alone in restaurants. During my early twenties, when I was single and living in Tokyo in the early 1990s, dates were rare, and I had the opportunity to spend a lot of time with myself. It was such a welcome relief from the dating world of college back in the US, as I got to be myself without anyone watching. I went to the movies, picking the film I wanted. I wandered museum halls, choosing the paintings I would sit in front of for hours. I slurped down bowls of ramen and got the last piece of sushi, never having to worry if I had seaweed in my teeth.

I took another sip of my margarita and remembered how much I loved that time in my life. On my days off from teaching, I took hikes, wandered bookstores, hung out in coffee shops, took a writing class, explored the city, and went to lots of movies. This is something I encourage to my life coach clients who come to me seeking love and looking to be in a relationship. I invite them to **date themselves**. To rediscover who they are, what they like and don't like, and spend time in their own company. When we are **comfortable in our own skin and like to spend time on our own**, I truly believe the dynamic is shifted when looking for a partner. We don't "need" another to have fun. We don't see having a partner as the only means of enjoyment.

Sitting there in the restaurant, I was grateful I had my note-book in my purse because it reminded me of all the times I had to wait. Waiting for my daughter's soccer practice to be over, my son's swim team practice to end, or a game or meet to start. So much waiting. I learned to **use that time as a gift**. Rather than passing the time, I used it. When everyone was back in the car and we were driving home, I wasn't seeking entertainment or joy. I created it with a pair of walking shoes, a good book, or a blank journal page.

Waiting for Kristal and Angela, I made a note to add more things to my purse so the next time I had an extra thirty minutes, I was able to do something I wanted and normally don't have time for.

"Sorry we are so late; I hope you didn't get bored."

"Are you kidding? I was sitting here reminiscing about living in Japan."

"I know you've told us before, but remind us: When you lived there, what were some of your best memories?"

I ordered another margarita and told them about all my times on my own, discovering parks, museums, Shinto shrines, and wandering and adventuring with me, myself, and I. The walk down memory lane reminded me of how much I love spending time by myself.

REFILL REFLECTION:

- When was the last time you took yourself on a date?
- Put it on the calendar and schedule a time with only yourself doing something fun, not a task you need to accomplish.

- Keep a tote in your car or fill your purse with items that bring you joy for the unexpected moments of waiting.
  - Similar to packing a snack, water bottle, or swim goggles for your kiddo, have your own items that inspire or bring joy.
- Use your next period of waiting to refuel.
  - Utilize this time to replenish and give yourself a taste of joy rather than festering in annoyance at biding your time.
- Rejuvenate by connecting to what delights you.
- Fill your Cup.

SIP 14.

LOVE YOU

———

*One person's "I love you" can mean nothing,
while another's "I love you" means the world.*

"What's your history of saying *I love you*?"

I was on retreat with my Anam Cara group, my faith circle of
six women for over ten years. We had decided this question
would be our dinner topic.

"My parents never said it."

"My family said it to each other every day, all the time."

We circled around, sharing our unique stories.

My turn arrived. When I was around ten, after giving me a
big hug I remember my mom saying, "You don't have to tell
me that you love me so much. You tell me too often."

I remember thinking she didn't tell me enough. At the age of
seventeen, I broke up with the nicest guy in the whole world

only because he told me he loved me after dating for one month. Married now for nearly twenty-five years, my husband and I waited six months to share the big L, and we now say it to each other at least once every other day. I tell strangers I love them after a heartfelt exchange, and some girlfriends hear it from me every time we are together and others only occasionally. I say "I love you" even when I know it won't be reciprocated because **if I'm feeling it, it must be expressed**. I only say it when I mean it, and in those moments when I feel it in my bones, I can't not say it. The feeling bubbles up within, and the only way out is to speak it. Otherwise, I'd wither up and blow away.

When our daughter was five, she hadn't told us she loved us, even though we spoke it to her all the time. Saying goodbye at the front door one day, my mother-in-law bent down to give her a hug and whispered sweetly, "I love you, honey."

"Thank you, Grandma."

"Whenever someone tells you they love you, you should say *I love you* back."

After the door closed behind her, I knelt down to her five-year-old level and said, "You only tell those you love back if you want to. Saying it back is not a requirement."

"I love you" means everything. "I love you" means nothing. We process and express this term of endearment in our own beautiful way. Some drop the "I," some say it more than once in one sentence, and for others **saying it once is everything**.

I invite my clients to look in the mirror and say "I love you" to themselves when they are challenged with seeking constant approval from others. I say it to myself regularly if I am down or in need of validation or encouragement. When I started doing this, **I released the incessant need to be liked and praised by others.** There are many mornings when I say, *"I love you, Jenny,"* right after my feet hit the floor, and I thank the day for showing up for me, yet again.

Raising me on her own, my mother's actions demonstrated her immense love for my siblings and me. She was gentle and kind, her love real and deep, but I craved words more than actions, too young to understand you can give love beyond words.

The time I lived in Japan, I learned the Japanese express love through action, not even having a word that translates to love like ours. This was before cell phones and email; I received letters to my Japanese address on the same day more than once from my mom and dad, even though they were sent from different cities. Their letters expressing love written uniquely, in their own style, slipped through the mail slot, landing next to each other.

I took my memories of how I received love into my own parenting practices. I thought I better say it a lot so our daughter knew she was loved down to her toes, as I didn't want her to think otherwise. In her tween years, we talked one night on my bed.

"How do you know I love you?"

She sat on the edge looking at her feet when she shared, "I just know. It doesn't matter how much you tell me. I feel it. It's a fact that you love me; I don't need to hear it all the time."

She wasn't me. I didn't have to overcompensate expressing my love with words because I didn't get the words I wanted when I was her age. This wasn't my childhood; it was hers. I learned to **ask what she wanted and needed**. What she wants and needs, of course, has morphed many times. In college now, she tells me in every conversation more than once that she loves me. I don't have any need to tell her she is telling me too much. **They are words that mean everything and nothing.**

You have your relationship and history of expressing love. What was the norm in your home growing up? Does your childhood experience bubble over into your parenting or other relationships? What is your experience of this personal, intimate, holy, and universal expression?

When do your people feel your love for them? It's a great conversation that can change and evolve as those you love change and evolve.

If I can learn to stand with others and not assume their needs but ask for what they need, a greater connection is built. As a parent, when I ask my children, I build a relationship with who they are. The path unfolds bumpy still, but it does not hold the bumps and pains of my own childhood.

REFILL REFLECTION:

- Are you hanging on to the past to define how and when "I love you" should be spoken?
- Are you honoring your kids' needs with these three words?
- Is it time to share your "I love you" story with your kids?

- Is it time to ask them theirs?
- Will you start telling yourself, "I love you"?
- Fill your Cup.

PART TWO

TRUTH

The voice of your mother, your inner critic, the ego, and the entire choir often become more than voices—they become **your truth**. These voices become the codes you plug into. As you practice connecting to your Cup and build a life-giving relationship with the wisdom that is there to support you, **what you tell yourself and what you believe matter**.

As you continue to hold everyone up in your world, notice the beliefs you carry. Do you hear what you tell yourself every day? Perhaps you believe you are the only one who can do certain tasks, and the fact that no one else is doing them is your proof. Your truth then becomes *I am alone in this; I'm unsupported.*

Flip that around and you may tell yourself you are fully supported and have great help with certain tasks, and the fact that you have asked for help and delegate is your proof. Your truth then becomes *I am fully supported; I'm not alone.*

Neither truth is good, bad, better, or wrong. These are truths I live, and so do you. Awareness about feeling stuck in your truth or changing it up and stepping into one that is **not depleting you but serving you** comes.

We tell ourselves stories all day long, and we believe them to be true. Even as I write this on the blank page, I am telling myself a story: *Who am I kidding? No one will read this book. Why am I bothering? I should stop.* Then I take a breath, remember why I began writing this book, and tell myself another story: *I have been wanting to do this and thinking about it forever. In this present season of my life, writing this book is my purpose. I want to share this book; I want others to grow and learn from my offerings. I want to continue to grow and learn, and writing this book is helping me do that. If I stop now, I will be sad that I gave up. I will be ignoring a big part of me.*

In the first four "Sips" of this section, I will be referencing the four principles Don Miguel Ruiz teaches us in his book *The Four Agreements*: **Be impeccable with your word; don't take anything personally; don't make assumptions; and always do your best.** For my own reference and teaching, I have taken the liberty to rename them: **Your word; not about you; ask instead; and standing tall or sitting down.**

Your truth may have some similarities to my truth, but each holds its own strength, weakness, guidance, mystery, promise, and light. We live by our **agreements and beliefs**. The little ones we tell ourselves each morning when our feet hit the floor and all the ones in between until we crawl into bed each night.

Yes, in each stage of your caretaking, your truth matters, and you are the only one who can tell your truth, believe it, and live it.

SIP 15.

YOUR WORD

———

*The rules you live by shape, mold, and
ultimately form your reality. The
agreements you make with yourself must
support, nurture, and align with your truth.*

"It won't. I promise," I told my son when he asked me if the
house would burn down. I tucked him into his top bunk and
kissed him one more time, knowing I would be back in his
room a few more times before the end of the evening.

Our son was six, a new kindergartner, his dad was traveling
a lot, the only grandfather he knew was dying, and we were
in the season of separation anxiety. A season that went on for
a number of years, but this was when I began to understand
that everything you said to our youngest kid meant gold.

Ruiz created essential principles out of Toltec wisdom that
support freer living. Every January I use these principles for
the first mini-retreat theme of the year with Mama Needs
a Refill, my restorative retreat business. We look at internal
agreements to live by that support our lives inside and out.

The first agreement Ruiz teaches us is "**Be impeccable with your word**." Your word is everything. Words carry the power to cut us down and build us up. One word can be the difference between life and death. Our son is wired to be a truth speaker. He says everything on his mind. At every age he has modeled speaking with kindness straight from his heart. When I made the promise to him that our house wouldn't burn down in the night, I actually didn't know if that was the truth. You bet I made sure all the candles were blown out and I checked the stove twice to make sure it was off before I went to bed. Then I said an extra prayer.

"Keep us safe; you heard my promise."

Obviously, I'm not going to tell a little boy who is worried about his house burning down before falling asleep, "Well, honey, we don't know; anything could happen."

I chose my words carefully. I knew my audience.

This is the balancing act we walk. What gets spoken and what stays withheld. I have learned when I mess up and don't speak with compassion, I leave a scar. This is when I go back and own up to my mistakes. I apologize for not showing up the way I would have liked. Kids at every age respond to this. Being parents doesn't mean we know what we are doing or that we do things the way we would like. We show up messy and unpracticed. Let your children see you unrehearsed and real. Human. Definitely not infallible. **Give yourself the grace to start over.** Pause and think about how you would like to proceed, and when you muck it up, go back and clean up the mess.

"I'm sorry" is worth gold.

When our truth speaker got older, I was afraid to always be 100 percent honest. One day, he called me out on my dancing around sincerity.

"Mom, quit pussyfooting and tell me."

Secretly, I was proud he knew such a great word to describe what I was feeling.

I took a breath.

"I'm afraid you'll be upset."

"Then I'll be upset."

That's exactly what I wanted to avoid. Another breath, this one much bigger than my first.

"The house could burn down one day; the earth is not flat; and your breath stinks."

Just kidding! That's not what I said. We ended up having the pussyfoot-honest conversation many times after that. My fear and intimidation were a big part of the problem. When I gave him a heads-up that I wanted to **speak honestly**, we avoided the yelling matches and ugly conversations. We found grace.

There is a time and a place for speaking candidly. Don't sugar-coat. Be straight. Deliver your message with kindness over passivity. Love over fear. Allow your words to be like little prayers.

People respond better when you trust them enough to be real with them. A great place to start acting impeccably with your word is noticing the promises and prayers you make to yourself. Be kind. Kind can be one word, or ten, or no words at all, as long as they are given as your truth.

REFILL REFLECTION:

- Notice what you say, how you say it, and when you say it.
- Are you speaking with kindness?
- Are you avoiding gossip?
- Are your words delivering a sword or an olive branch?
- How do you talk to yourself?
- Are you owning up and taking responsibility?
- Fill your Cup.

SIP 16.

NOT ABOUT YOU

—

The water off a duck's back isn't theirs
to keep as it beads off their feathers.

She didn't call me; she called her dad. At first, that really hurt.

Our daughter was away at college, and our mother-daughter relationship had blossomed. We both agreed on her last visit home that we did better over the phone and apart. (For right now.) She had been applying for summer internships, and we had spoken over a video chat the day before. That morning I sent her a "good luck" text, and she messaged me back, "Thank you."

When I heard her sweet voice coming from her dad's office that afternoon, I fought the urge to run in and see her face. I stood in the hallway listening to their FaceTime conversation. She had a great interview and wanted to know if she should send a thank you email and, if so, how to word it. Her dad gave great counsel. But wait, *I'm the writer in the family. I'm the one with the English degree, and her dad always comes to me for thank you email edits and feedback.*

I walked slowly into the room and sat behind her dad, doing my best to button my lip. After a few minutes of feeling excited for her and unable to resist the urge, the button popped.

"Lead with that, don't wait until tomorrow, be sure to include…" the jar of unsolicited advice dumped on the table.

"Thanks, Mom."

"Don't take anything personally," is Don Miguel Ruiz's second agreement. If you have never allowed someone else's look, words, or actions to affect you, then I want to know your secret. Out of his four principles, personal codes to live by, this has been my biggest struggle for most of my life. I want to belong. I want to matter. After my parents' divorce, I feared abandonment. What I didn't realize is when I allowed the words, facial expressions, and interpretations of another's actions to be my truth, my confidence, self-esteem, and love for myself was wounded. This carried on to parenthood.

"You don't understand," stung, knowing full well the words of a teenager often sting.

"You love her better," slapped, knowing full well at one time, I believed the same about my own siblings.

And speaking of siblings, I used to get my panties all in a bundle and grow a spiky tail when one of my siblings said, "You had it easier than we did. Dad was out of the house for you."

I don't need to describe the load of feelings that brings up or the emotional mark of that memory. I can only imagine your own experience of a wounded heart from another's turn of phrase. This is why this principle is so critical to our healing. I would tell our son, our speaker of truth, every day from ages five to seventeen, "Water off a duck's back," when he came home from school hurt by the words of a classmate, friend, teacher, or coach. These were opportunities to find something else to do with the wounds the words opened. To find self-approval, self-confidence, and self-love.

Their label, expression, opinion, perspective, remark, or glance wasn't about him. Nor is it about me when I am the receiver of a word that hurts or triggers. It is about the other person. *Holding up a mirror.* Our son, now eighteen, and me, midfifties, finally get it. We care what others think. This is our wiring. We allow another's opinions to become our truth. There comes the point where it **wounds more to put energy and give any weight to what others do and say** than to work on releasing it. I truly believe that others are going through their own story and beliefs, spewing what they unconsciously think and feel about their stuff. It gets interpreted as ours.

After years of our son coming home from school annoyed and wounded by others, he now tells me, "Water off a duck's back, Mom." I smile, hearing my words from years ago, walking him to the bus stop. That's right, *I don't have to take it personally. It's not about me.*

"I wonder what's going on with them?" he suggests.

And to think, when he was in one of his tantrums, and my husband would say, "Like mother, like son."

I would get my panties all in a bundle. And I took it personally.

"Yes, lucky kid," I now can quip.

Think about all the times you have been wounded by another—their message, their silence, breathing it all in like it was yours. You play these messages in your mind, forming and shaping your opinions and actions toward yourself. The words spoken are actually coming from the deliverer's own wounded heart. Not only teenagers but all of us can throw daggers with our eyes, our pointed words, and ill-intentioned statements.

Nosing my way into my daughter and husband's conversation that afternoon, my buttoned lip popped open one last time.

"I want to acknowledge that I do this to the two of you. I barge in on your phone time."

"Yes, you do," she was quick to respond.

"I take full responsibility," I continued, "I'm sorry."

I don't even remember her response because I was taking her quick reply personally. But this time without tears or blame. I quietly went to my office and pulled out my journal. I filled the blank page. Afterward, the clouds parted in my mind, and I saw the situation differently. I saw it from her eyes. That is how I found peace. The hurt now replaced with understanding. The wound my opportunity for growth.

Do you relate? Are you willing to find peace and understanding rather than taking things personally?

Water off a duck's back. Can you put on your repellent feather coat?

REFILL REFLECTION:

- Where are you allowing another's opinion or truth to be yours?
- Can you imagine what they are going through?
- Where can "water off a duck's back" help you move on?
- Pull out your journal, acknowledge the hurt, and leave it on the page.
- Fill your Cup.

SIP 17.

ASK INSTEAD

—

Like Mom says, "Don't be an ass."

"I arrive to work early most days, and every time I walk by my boss's office, she says 'hello' back to me but never with a smile. I watch her greet others with a big wide grin. I don't think she likes me, or I have done something to make her mad."

There are countless conversations I have with clients who come to me thinking someone doesn't like them or is mad at them. One client, I will call her Abby Assumption, thought her boss didn't like her because every morning when they greeted each other the boss had "evil eyes."

The third agreement Ruiz offers is **"Don't make assumptions."** This one alone clears up so many communication issues. The pot has been stirred of unresolved feelings, and we are sitting in the stew of old stories, traumas, dramas, and painful memories. In that regard, an assumption is a gift because it reminds you of what still needs to be healed. It leaves room for possibility.

I challenged Abby to hold a different story in her head and to give something different a try. She accepted the challenge. Before she went to work each morning, she took some extra time in her car to remind herself that she was likable. (Cue the *Saturday Night Live* skit featuring Al Franken as Stuart Smalley, the character who was known to say, "I'm good enough, I'm smart enough, and doggone it, people like me.") She envisioned her boss smiling back at her like she did with her colleagues. It took courage, and a few more weeks went by when Abby asked her boss for a meeting.

"I want to touch base. I feel uncomfortable asking, but I am curious. I sense a different energy between us. Am I doing the job you expect? Specifically, are you satisfied with my role here? I want to make sure this is working out on your end."

Her boss was surprised and softened at the question. "Please don't tell me you are thinking of quitting?"

"Absolutely not. Frankly, I wasn't sure what you thought of me."

This opened up a conversation. Turns out her boss was in the middle of a divorce and had a lot of stress at home. She didn't come out and explain why she didn't smile at Abby in the morning or even acknowledge the assumption any further. Something more important happened.

"My boss smiled at me three times this week, and during our review she gave me a raise."

Abby's relationship with her boss and their interactions went on to grow and change in a number of positive ways. Instead of assuming, Abby asked questions. Rather than carrying the belief that she wasn't liked, she took control of what she believed about herself.

We won't understand everyone, and everyone won't understand us. When we are triggered and our beliefs challenged, we make assumptions. The only way forward out of the assumption loop is to *stop*. Ask. **Be curious.** Listen and engage with wonder instead of blame. That's what this principle teaches us. **We can't know for sure unless we actually inquire.**

In our long-standing relationships, we think we know what the other is thinking, and we strongly believe we can predict their every move, thought, response, and behavior. Often this is true. However, I believe this assumption is unfair and puts people in a box with a label on it. People do change, and it's often our assumptions that cause the friction in the first place.

If you aren't already, start asking. Begin your interaction **without an assumption and with a question**:

- "Do you care if...?"
- "I know you do this every day, but tell me, will you be making coffee in the morning?"
- "Here's what's going on with me. Do you want to tell me what's going on with you?"

I had another client who said her child never talks to her. When I inquired about the backstory, it was clear why the child never talked. The mom was always talking.

"What if you withhold sharing and questioning every day after school and leave room for your child to talk if they want to?"

She did this. You can probably imagine what transpired. When the mom allowed spaciousness and didn't fill it with talking, her child slowly started saying more.

Basing our actions, words, and thoughts on assumptions creates a big chasm between us and others. We must begin the habit of asking questions. **Ask** to clarify. **Ask** to know for sure. Asking shows you are listening, caring, and engaged.

LEAVE ROOM FOR CHANGE.

Assuming—most of us do it. Imagine if we didn't. There may be fewer asses in the world, huh?

REFILL REFLECTION:

- Ask the question before you assume.
- Be curious as if you haven't been in this same situation a hundred times before.
- Notice the automatic assumptions you make on a daily basis:
  - "She will be mad."
  - "He will be quiet."
- Leave room for possibility.
- Fill your Cup.

STANDING TALL OR SITTING DOWN

———

The opposite of comparison is truth, and when you are standing in your truth there is absolutely no room to compare.

"I used to run marathons."

"I used to make art every weekend."

"Meditation is not happening like it used to."

These are comments from three different clients. I invited them to put away the measuring stick and show up to their present body, mind, and spirit. No excuses and no complaints, getting present to what the body can do now, the mind can hold, and spirit is open to receive. That is the same way to apply the idea of living in balance: no comparison to yesterday, another version of yourself, or to another person.

And in Ruiz's final agreement, **"Always do your best,"** a bow is tied on all the four principles, uniting them together with integrity. Your best yesterday can look radically different than today's best, based on circumstance and honestly **checking in with yourself** on what is possible in that moment. Showing up is often the very best you can do. This often means letting go of your ideal to get it all done or as well as you did it yesterday. Tuning in to what you can do, physically, mentally, emotionally, and spiritually will better support you. I invite you to come to peace with the fact that letting go of every demand, recognizing only so much can happen in one day, and sometimes a moment to rest serves you far more than accomplishing one more task. Comparing your deeds and actions against another is a very slippery slope. There is no way up, so release comparison and trust you are doing the very best you can.

LIFE ISN'T A RACE.
Helpful questions I ask myself to determine balance and doing my best for that particular task, situation, or day:

1. What must happen next?
2. What can I honor?
3. If I were to end the day, what task, activity, or action must reach completion?
4. Can I live with "X" happening tomorrow?
5. What is the best way to love myself or another with the time and energy I have right now?
6. What can I let go of?
7. What feels best?

Choose the question that serves you or ask another one. You are not in the past; you are not in the anticipated and uncharted future. You are here. Right now. Do you sit down or stand tall?

Both the right answer, depending on the day, what's in your tank, and what needs to be honored.

All three clients were in new stages. For one client, life before kids meant lots of time to train for marathons. Life during kids meant she was in the season of survival, and running for sanity and stress relief was key and shorter runs sufficed. This eventually morphed into discovering other forms of exercise to honor the hardwired need for a challenge when she hit the next season. The artist client was in need of new inspiration and took a class to honor her curiosity and thirst for more. Her curiosity led to a whole new interest that turned into a career, and her weekends now included rest over productivity. The meditating client's practice was completely abandoned during the COVID-19 pandemic, her focus elsewhere but still having the desire to be still. By modifying her meditation practice, she discovered that ten minutes was not only more doable but also produced the same result of meditating twice a day for twenty minutes.

Honor the season you are in, both with those you care for and with your particular needs. Different needs can determine your season. Although the demands on you can define your mental, emotional, physical, and spiritual capacity, creating balance is very much about what you are capable of in the present.

REFILL REFLECTION:

- You don't even have to ask, "What does my best look like today?" Instead, ask, "What can I hold today?"
- Choose one of the four agreements to practice for a week.
  - Write an agreement from "Sip" 15, 16, 17, or 18 on a sticky note and put it on your bathroom mirror or save it as the wallpaper on your cell phone.
- Notice if you are choosing agreements that support you.
- Fill your Cup.

LET IT GO

———

*Your little quirky habits are often
covering up a bigger issue.*

My addiction was pillows—not buying them, hording them, or sniffing them, but arranging them. Sounds innocent enough and harmless, and that's true, but this constant preoccupation of mine has personal truth buried in the story of my obsessive tidying-up behavior. The truth is I was trying to make myself matter and be useful.

What's your ingrained habit that is slightly neurotic, doesn't hurt anyone, and has lulled you into thinking it gives you sanity and peace of mind? Please tell me I'm not alone.

As a little girl growing up in a chaotic home with my dad hidden away in his bedroom, spending his days reading and smoking, straightening up my environment gave me a sense of safety and order. Tidying provided a sense of peace and comfort that continued to be the only thing I believed I could control as an adult, as it gave me a sense of accomplishment to step into a room that was neat and tidy. As an adult, besides a sense of order and a sense of control, my pillow-fluffing addiction became the way I ignored the matters of my heart.

A matter of the heart is anything calling your name. It calls you in a loving way, wanting your time and attention. I allowed menial tasks like arranging the pillows on the couch, beds, and chairs around the house to distract me and keep me from my matters of the heart.

Can you relate? Do you catch yourself doing a task that doesn't need to be done or can simply wait, but it provides a sense of accomplishment so you do it automatically? Is this task keeping you from the things you wish you had time for or that you long to do?

If prioritizing your little quirky habit has gotten ridiculous like mine had, **start small**. Notice you're going toward the little task that brings order to your environment or a perceived peace of mind and try this practice instead:

GET REAL:
- Stop. Ask, "Am I doing this to avoid something I truly wish I had time to do?"
- Be honest.
- If no: carry on with the task.
- If yes: bravo. Now ask what is one thing you can do right now, as you put down the distraction, be it a pillow, alphabetized soup can, or crumb on the counter? And no judgment if you notice you've already done this task today. This is a new moment to seize. (There will always be crumbs.)

- Now, take your answer and do it for the same amount of time the menial task would take.
- One minute of breathing. Thirty seconds of doodling, one yoga pose, laughing, singing, or smelling flowers will carry you further.

Perhaps repositioning the living room pillows more than five times a day isn't your jam, but what is the thing that has become habit that makes you feel like you're doing something when in actuality you are avoiding a matter of **your heart**?

Notice your unconscious habit and be curious about its nature. There is a fine line between tidiness, obsessiveness, and avoidance. The answer could be hidden in asking yourself a thought-provoking question about the slightly neurotic behavior you believe you *must* do. Create a question that works for you to get underneath the motivation for the action. The question for me was, What am I avoiding? Firstly, that question helped me to become aware of what I was doing. I was trying to make myself useful and give myself a purpose in that moment.

Secondly, I was unconsciously attaching to perfection—the false sense of perfection because there is no such thing. The appearance of order in my home gave me a sense of control as I attached to things looking organized and tidy. Underneath this outside appearance was detachment from what I was avoiding. The things I was **avoiding** were not only the very things calling my name, but they were also the things that were my **fuel**—not the tidiness and flawlessly arranged pillows.

What has become your excuse and ultimately your default to ignoring and resisting your fuel? Do you have a natural tendency to care for everything and everyone else before caring for yourself because, frankly, it's so much easier than attending to your own care? If everything and everyone else is handled, is there a distraction getting in your way of shining a light on what's underneath the false sense of control or perfection? What is drawing you away from your heart's desire?

Get clear on that matter of your heart. Moving your body, using your mental capacity, expressing your feelings, connection, or something else. Once you are clear on your heart matter notice the distraction, the minutia that **draws you away from honoring it**. Your own version of pillow addiction. Maybe the kitchen counters need to be spotless before you can sit down in the evening. Maybe all your canned goods in the cupboard need to be alphabetized before you can close the door. I get it. Notice your distraction and start letting it go, and notice no one dies when your counter has a crumb on it or the can of tuna is next to the peanut butter and the labels are not facing outward.

There is nothing wrong with your behavior. It's incredibly normal to distract and resist, but how is it serving you? Notice if this task truly gives you peace or if it minimizes the time you spend fueling up. You need that fuel, and still a natural tendency to resist it can show up. Pay attention to how you feel at the end of the day. Are you wishing you called a friend or painted a picture, and instead, you have an arranged cupboard that gives you no peace at all? It's like you fueled up with the wrong type of gas. That longing is a clue into your heart matter—your specific kind of fuel.

Ultimately, you don't have control of the stuff on the outside. Someone will reach for the can of tuna and turn the label the "wrong" way. You do have control over how long you spend doing that activity or whether you reserve it for tomorrow and address the heart matter first.

Listen to the whisper, whether it's to write, read, dance, or sing before the distracting behavior keeps you from it. Don't be lulled into thinking that distraction makes you the perfect person or useful. Don't be tricked. Avoid the mind game and do the thing that actually gives you fuel.

REFILL REFLECTION:

- Is it time to change a habit that has become your excuse into a habit that refuels?
- What's one of your neuroses that's getting in your way and taking over what really matters to you?
- Are you willing to begin doing this habit less, toss it cold turkey, or replace it with something life-giving?
- I dare you to fill your Cup.

SIP 20.

TEAM FAMILY

———

We are together for a reason;
we need each other.

—MY HUSBAND, ROB MCGLOTHERN

"Okay, Cousin Julia is getting married today, and you are the ring bearer and flower girl," my niece Katherine said to her two young cousins. "She needs our help. Are you ready to help out?"

When our kids were little, ages five and two and a half, to keep the peace at a family wedding, my adult niece Katherine circled up her little cousins and asked if they could help her sister's wedding go smoothly.

She turned her attention to the younger cousins, who didn't have a role but were the siblings of the two with responsibilities.

"Yes," came the gleeful chorus.

To seal the deal, on the count of three, they were instructed to shout out, "Team family!" Running amuck ceased as they dutifully obliged. Not only did this motto help high energy at a family event, but it also continued to be the saving grace of our family of four for years to come.

During road trips, family arguments, disconnection, challenges, or anticipatory joy on all levels, when one of us says, "Family on three," even now with one family member in college, with fists touching in a united circle we dutifully show up to one another and reply, "Team family!"

When they were little, it eased tension. As they are older, it provides humor and a **tangible reminder** that we can let bickering go, get on the same page, and be there for one another.

Do you have something that calls you all together? Would a simple phrase unite you all and serve as a reminder of what matters?

Before the summer of 2013 kicked into full gear at our house, the husband and I decided to have a family meeting. As I'm wired to have a plan to ease my anxiety and have control to retain my sanity, I recognized the need to bring in the whole family. As much as I like things done a certain way, I would rather have help than have it done perfectly.

"I'll hang up my suit and towel when we get home every day."

"I'll pack my swim bag and make my lunch."

"I'll pack the snacks."

"I'll take out the dog before we leave each morning."

Even when kids are young, a simple job empowers their sense of worth and contribution. I was delighted with how quickly the list of responsibilities got taken care of as both kids took their jobs seriously. If you feel your control tentacles getting itchy, take stock in building your **children's empowerment**. Getting out the door will be easier if your child recognizes their purpose in this endeavor.

Years later, after early morning summer swim team practice was no longer a part of our lives, as we were all loading up the car for a road trip, our son reminded us of our family motto. A couple of us behind schedule, a couple of us grouchy, one of us mad, and one of us annoyed, we piled into the car.

"Sorry, everyone, for getting upset. We are going to have a great trip. Team family on three?"

"Team family on three," a couple of us responded.

"One, two, three."

"Team family!" we all said in unison.

Will you give delegation a try? Will you notice that the family who comes together on three and pitches in not only helps with your sanity but everyone's? Make an effort not to do it all, ask for what you need, put in the practice of not doing everything, and trust the unfolding. This family of yours is not an accident. You have found each other and created this unit for reasons way beyond your comprehension. As you bump up against one another, count to three on your own, and then together.

Every time I'm amazed at the response and unity, and every time I ask one of them afterward to take out the garbage.

REFILL REFLECTION:

- Your family is your team, and it is easy to rub each other the wrong way and piss each other off.
- Taking on the attitude that you are the only one who can do everything invites an empty Cup and more chaos.
- Where can you ask for help?
- Where can you let go of control?
- Are you willing to empower your kids by letting them discover what they are capable of doing?
- Where can you surrender and simply allow?
- Fill your Cup.

SIP 21.

NOT MY CIRCUS

—

Energy is contagious.

"Mary, honey, don't hop on their roller coaster; it's their ride, not yours."

This sage advice was passed down by my dear friend's mom, Maureen. Mary was caught up in one of her three kid's angst, when her mom reminded her to keep her feet on the ground. One moment a kid is up, the next down, a continual loop riding all the emotions, and this warning was to not join in on the exhausting, everchanging amusement park ride.

"It will change soon enough," Maureen comforted.

How true, this encouraging caution. In the next moment, there will be a new emotion. The emotions we all experience change hundreds of times in one day.

"Not my circus, not my monkeys." My daughter has taken on this phrase as a college student, juggling teachers', friends', and coworkers' energy. People go to her for advice and support.

At one point it took a toll, until she realized their frustration can't be added on to her own problems and concerns. If someone in her circle was having a problem, she had to learn to not take it on as her own. She learned how to draw the line. It's about honoring her needs, creating a boundary, saying no, and having an outlet. She has running, working out, and healthy friendships to turn to for balancing out the negative, demanding energy in her life.

Getting caught up in the drama of others is easy. We care. They are our family and our friends, and their happiness and well-being matter greatly to us. The problem arises when we take on their energy. Their upset or hurt becomes ours. They storm into the room mad at a teacher, and we want to call the teacher and resolve the situation, now. Their tears become our own. It's a challenge to not take on the struggles of those we love. We want to pluck a cure out of the sky and make it all better. Not to mention, we are worn out as their emotions feel like ours.

Fear holding them captive becomes our fear. When we hop on the ride with them, or we are the one wrangling monkeys, we are escalating the situation. What is really needed and would support them more is if we did the opposite. Be the roller coaster engineer on the ground rather than the passenger next to them in the empty seat. In their dizzying spin, when we remain rooted and the calm in the storm this helps them more than anything.

Whether it's positive or negative, energy is so infectious it can shift the climate in a room in an instant. One person can have the power to cause everyone in the room to tense up or to relax. One person's energy can ignite others to start singing and dancing a happy tune or inspire them to reach for a window to let in more air for the overpowering negativity to escape. I am that powerful, and so are you. Energy spreads like wildfire. One person's sadness becomes another's, and the same can be said about joy.

When our son was little, I often hopped on the roller coaster. It would begin with me wanting to control, stop, and change his tantrum, frustration, or sadness. Between the ages of two and eleven, not a day would go by that he would not cry or explode all over the room, his emotions filling every nook and cranny. Concerned about his sadness and worried about his outbursts, I carried fear in every action I made and every word I spoke.

Would he inherit my dad's chronic depression? Would he grow out of his mood swings? Who else will understand his volatile, fragile nature? While everyone was labeling him sensitive, it was me who was feeling sensitive and protective. I was feeling his feelings, and he was feeling mine. Energy is wordless, carrying a mighty spark.

When my friend Mary shared her mom's wisdom with me, she was witness to one of our youngest's dramatic mood swings. She saw my frustration, sadness, worry, and fear. She reminded me I had a choice. I could keep riding with him, set off by his upset and turning it into my worry, or I could stay on the ground and be anchored.

When your child is yelling, hitting, and bouncing off the walls and won't come down from the ceiling, it's hard not to go up there with them. I get it. When your teen is yelling at you, it's easy to feel like you have no control over the situation. When a stranger in traffic cuts you off, your partner has a bad day, or your colleague snaps at you, remember **it's not about you**. You don't want anyone to be mad at you; you want your loved ones to be happy, healthy, and at peace.

Can you allow others to feel their big feelings without breathing them in as your own? Can you allow while resisting reaction? When their loud and intense energy rubs off on you, remember "Not your circus," be in the audience, and grab a seat. **Breathe, watch, allow, and breathe again. Let the ride circle around you.**

Feel your feet on the ground and breathe. If you're calm, you can't amplify the charged-up energy in the room from your child, partner, coworker, loved one, or friend. If you want them to feel calm, safe, and peaceful, you must feel that way first, and doing so begins with **detaching from their crazy and finding your breath**. Give yourself a good boundary, protect yourself from breathing in their toxic vibe, and choose to spread a different vibe, one that supports and nurtures the both of you. Instead of matching their energy, see if they will match yours. Breathe in calm so you can both breathe out calm.

Something that helps me immensely is to remember **one person's emotions is for their work, their life, their story, and their lesson**. If I try to change their emotions, I am robbing them of their learning. Similarly, your emotions are for you to unravel and ultimately learn and grow from. Yes, learning from your emotions will take practice, but you can do it.

You can also step out of the room; take the space you need. This works with all ages and all people. No pointing or blaming. Take ownership for what you need and your own energy. Your energy isn't perfect, either. Check it before you connect with others. Notice when you need a snack, a mood adjustment, a moment to yourself, or a break of any kind, and take it.

We all feed off each other. Often, an adjustment to the thermometer is needed. We need each other, so step off the ride if you feel yourself getting caught up. Let them know you love them and you need some space to catch your breath. You get to wave your hand, step off the roller coaster, and move on over to the slow train, the one with a seat belt, a guardrail, and a different view. With your feet on the ground, inhale and exhale.

REFILL REFLECTION:

- Think about a person in your life who triggers you.
- Chances are, you trigger them too.
- How can you shift your energy when engaging with this individual?
- Can you let go of blame, choose a different vibration, and be responsible for the energy you bring into the room?
- Fill your Cup.

SUPERHERO

———

*Because you're capable doesn't
mean you have to do everything.*

"Sure, I'll do it."

As I was agreeing to be a room parent for the second year in a row, I was already pissed. Pissed I was asked and pissed at myself for being so damn "nice."

"Okay, you bet."

Now, this time I was agreeing to organize a women's group I had absolutely no desire to organize.

It's like I have Tourette's, but instead of saying "Fuck" I say "Yes." Okay, you caught me, I say both.

If you, too, are hardwired like Wonder Woman to answer thirty emails, send three texts, scramble eggs, and plan a fundraising event, all while dodging flaming bullets, driving carpool, and writing your dissertation, it doesn't mean you have to. Even if you're capable and quite known amongst your peers for getting shit done all before many have had their first cup of coffee, you get to say, "No, thanks."

Perhaps part of you enjoys being hyperproductive while the other part wishes you weren't so willing. The unwilling part is the very real piece of you that ends the day utterly exhausted with a plan to burn your cape. Do you want to learn how to stop taking on so much and to respond to what needs you have in the moment instead of what you think you should be doing?

It all starts with saying *yes* or *no* **for the right reasons and not overextending yourself,** even when you have a lot of energy and wherewithal. Don't agree to something if the reasons you're saying *yes* don't outweigh what you're giving up.

Ask yourself if you will feel overtaxed as the Neighborhood Watch Organizer for the fifth year in a row, tired of herding cats, exhausted with all those late nights working on a project no one else agreed to take on, or frustrated with repeatedly helping out a friend. When saying *yes* equates to more mess, drama, stress, and spreading your energy too thin, it's time to practice the power of *no*. It's time for a boundary. **You are the only one who can set this boundary.** Recognize where a line needs to be drawn.

Overtaxed, exhausted, and annoyed are all things you can get over, but feeling that way repeatedly builds up and leaves a nasty mark of resentment and can lead to serious burnout. When you're asked to do something and a *yes* or *no* is requested, turn to this method:

YES OR NO?:

- Place a hand on your gut or heart. Take a breath. (See "Sip 3" for a breath refresher if necessary.)
- If the answer can wait, tell the person seeking your help, "Give me a day to get back to you." Consult all parts of you—body, mind, and spirit—for your true answer. (For a full discernment explanation of how to do this, see "Sip 29.")
- If the answer can't wait, take another breath and ask yourself: *Do I have the bandwidth for this request?* If saying *yes* feels authentic, possible, and relatively good, that is your answer. If you clearly receive the answer as *no*, stick with that. Look said person directly in the eye and say, "Thank you for thinking of me. I must pass for the sanity of everyone." You aren't obliged to explain why or to share all you have going on in your life right now. *No* is *no*. And *no* is not rude, unkind, disrespectful, or selfish. *No* is a healthy, often necessary, life-giving boundary.

Saying *yes* when you don't want to *is* rude, unkind, and disrespectful. The energy that goes with the unwilling *yes* is toxic. **No is a loving boundary,** yet women are raised believing it's a bad word and that we must agree to it all, that it's our job to say *yes*. What if you modeled for your children, demonstrated to your friends, and showed your coworkers and partners that *no* is an empowering and life-giving word?

Let's get on the same page about the meaning of bandwidth. Yes, we get it, *you are capable*, but each day, each week, each month, and while we are at it, each year, you can only "do" so much. Life throws you curveballs you can't control, and you do have quite a bit of control over how you respond to others requests on your time and energy.

When a client tells me they feel guilty for not doing more or helping out a friend in need for the billionth time, I tell them to remember when they say *no* that empowers the other to find another *yes*. Saying *no* is an invitation for the other to rely on their own strength or to lean on someone who does have the bandwidth.

You won't lose a good friend; you will gain sanity. I invite you to tuck your cape into your yoga pants and carry on.

REFILL REFLECTION:

- You're wired to handle, solve, fix, and do it all. This can leave you depleted.
- Let's try some effective rewiring.
- How do you want to respond to the needs of others and to life?
- What new responses are you willing to practice with the goal of being fulfilled and not being overextended?
- Where can you create a life-giving boundary?
- Fill your Cup.

SIP 23.

CLEAN SLATE

"Should" is the strange glue that keeps
you stuck to the floor, buying into
guilt, and emptying your Cup.

I stepped into my guilty slippers one Saturday morning as I chose to stay home from yoga for absolutely the most ridiculous reason. I listened to *should* when I knew better. You've done this too, I know it. Do you know *should* is an illusion fabricated in your mind? Knowing this, do you still want to eat it for breakfast?

Let's shine a bright light on *should* and put it to bed as you allow me to share a story that may sound familiar, and in the following "Sip," we will toss those guilty slippers. Pay attention to where I'm speaking your story, your experience, and your belief patterns.

One Friday night, I made the plan to attend the next morning's Bikram yoga class, which fit perfectly with my schedule and the family activities. I had set a goal of attending yoga three times a week; this class was my only opportunity to round out this three-class commitment to myself.

My bones ached for the curative powers of a one-hundred-and-ten-degree heated studio. My skin longed to sweat out all the toxins I'd been consuming—both literally and figuratively, not to mention the nightly peanut butter binges—in the hopes of dissolving frustration, overwhelm, and stress. My limbs ached to be stretched, my mind to be emptied, and my spirit to bask in the connection I received standing half-naked in front of a mirror in a room with thirty strangers. I wanted to go to that class with every bone and ligament in my body.

My downfall was assessing the family's mood. One look at the scene in the living room: Daughter played quietly, son happily focused on his drawing, and husband contentedly reading the newspaper. There was no fighting; laughter and general peace on the home front set the stage—even our dog, Buford, was snoring at my husband's feet. How could any mother in her right mind leave this Norman Rockwell setting? Yep, I went down that path. I actually believed I *should* stay home because everyone was content.

Have you done this? Do you talk yourself out of something because you *think* no other mother in their right mind would leave a happy family to do something for herself?

Convincing myself that weekends *should* be about family, choosing to skip yoga was the beginning of everything going downhill. You can fill in the details with your own tale of caving into *should* and having everything turn upside down.

"Should" generates in your head, not your heart. It comes from a place of overthinking and analyzing to the point of dismissing all desire and longing. If you equate time away from your family, especially when they're little, as being a neglectful parent then perhaps it's time to examine and understand that *should* carries deep roots.

Your personal relationship with this powerful auxiliary verb has a history arising from your mother's voice, her mother's voice before her, and in fact, tracing back through all your female ancestors. *Should* also carries weight from your father's voice, and his father's voice, and so on.

"This is how it's done in our family."

You've created your own *should* belief system based on family patterns—or in defiance of them. "Mom never exercised on a Saturday when we were home, so I *should* follow suit." Or, "Mom never did anything for herself when we were home on the weekend, and look where it got her. I *shouldn't* repeat that pattern."

I offer you a fresh perspective when it comes to how you make decisions, leaving the voices of the past where they belong, in the past. Forget your mother's ways, obliterate your father's beliefs, and take a good, long look at your own ways and convictions. You *get* to decide how to **navigate to your own truth**. This is your opportunity to operate from a clean slate, one that isn't tarnished by how you were raised. You're not your parents, and your children aren't you.

To get past ingrained patterns, **substitute "should" with "must."** "What *must* I do? How *must* I be? What *must* I say?" Feel the difference? *Must* carries urgency and conviction without shaking a finger in your face as shame is no longer invited to the party. When you've tuned in with *must*, the judgmental voice is quieted, and you're plugged into your wise guide who is ready to speak up.

Think of it this way: *Should* is the stepsister who pops by unannounced, but you're the one who let her in. Now, she'll control your decisions, pester you with unwelcome advice and opinions, and bully you into sabotage as you continue to ignore what you *must* do. *Should* ignites thoughts like, "Well, I'm home all day. I *should* be the one to do all the laundry, have the house orderly, have the hot meal on the table, get my exercise in when the kids are at school, and take care of my needs when it's convenient for everyone else."

Instead, ask what *must* you do. *Must* feeds the fire that wants to nurture, balance, and provide care for you so you can care for others without burnout and frustration.

Do you feel the difference between the two? Try it.

Use a version of the *Yes or No* method from "Sip 22" by placing your hand on your gut or heart and ask your question. In the example of doing for yourself on a Saturday morning, ask, "What *must* I do to care for myself today?"

Choose wisely and quit giving the excuse that you have all these other things to do, things you *should* do before considering your needs. The only rule book is the one you've written in your mind based on your personal history, ideals, and perceptions. You're the only one who can discover the real truth in your happiness, and often that means separating yourself from an old story or out-moded guidelines.

If you reposition yourself to *must* instead of *should*, your true needs will be met. **For it is in ignoring your needs that your Cup is emptied.** You *must* get in the habit of asking yourself daily, "What do I need?"

On that Saturday, I could've asked myself that very question and removed *should* from the equation. I opened myself up to frustration instead and got pissy with my family. I was actually frustrated with myself. I was the only one to blame for the emptiness I experienced for having scorned my yoga commitment. I ended the day not having cared for my needs, so when others needed me, I was resentful, short-tempered, and a total butthead. I stayed home to avoid guilt, and in the end, I felt far worse.

Start tuning into what you need, and the *must* will become clear. On an individual basis, it may look something like this: connection, creative expression, laughter, movement, music, rest, touch, or quiet. This translates into what you *must* do: meet a friend for coffee, write, watch *Jimmy Kimmel Live!*, go for a walk, turn on Van Morrison, put your feet up on the couch, ask for a hug, or close your eyes while wearing noise-canceling headphones.

Watch yourself turn into a completely different person after honoring your *must*. And watch everyone around you transform. Clear the slate, tune in, and be attentive to your own needs as this creates a far more authentic, life-giving Norman Rockwell moment on a Saturday morning—even if you aren't pictured in the scene.

REFILL REFLECTION:

- Stop dismissing your soul-filling needs as futile.
- Be aware of how often you use the word *should*.
- Play with replacing *should* with *must*.
- Notice what changes when you begin to eliminate *should* in your life.
- Fill your Cup.

SIP 24.

ELEPHANT IN THE ROOM

Guilt is such a great excuse, isn't it?

If *should* is the relative who comes over without an invitation, *guilt* is the one who moves in, sleeps on the couch, and never leaves because no one kicks him out. I have noticed in my life, as well as in the lives of my friends and clients, that *guilt* is the excuse that makes it easy to avoid truly honoring our needs. Guilt can keep you stuck while secretly making you feel okay about it. The *guilt* badge is worn like a decorated medal in both cases of not doing for yourself and in making yourself a priority.

How many times have you used *guilt* as an excuse to not take care of your needs or let *guilt* be part of your self-care story?

"I would go away this weekend with girlfriends, but Saturday my son has his piano lesson. I feel bad not taking him since I'm the one who makes him go in the first place."

Choosing to not attend something for your child because you feel *guilty* if you don't is different than choosing to attend because you want to. **Choose with your heart.**

Something that shapes your decisions as a mother is *guilt* and, like *should*, it very possibly is something passed down from your own mother. *Guilt* happens to be second cousin of *should*, so closely related to each other, yet often unaware of the thread of shared similarity. *Guilt* is front and center when I'm talking with friends, family, clients, retreat attendees, and strangers about self-care. Women often feel obliged to share their reasons.

"I feel bad not going to her recital, but it is the only time I could schedule a massage."

Your reasons are your reasons, own them and please know the *guilty* feeling can get passed on. Remember how energy is contagious? **No one needs to understand your choice but you.**

Think about it: *Guilt* is your motivator for action as well as inaction. You often do things for others because you feel *guilty*—but you *don't* do things for yourself because it makes you feel *guilty*. Do you hear how truly twisted and messed up that is?

I knew better on that Norman Rockwell Saturday morning I shared in the previous "Sip," but out of habit and regular conditioning, I was certain *guilt* would take over if I went to yoga class. "What kind of mother am I to leave such a good thing all for a good sweat?" Turns out not going was far worse than the *guilt* I thought I would experience for leaving a happy family or the *guilt* I did experience for wanting to leave them.

Guilt sabotages plans and takes over rational thought. There are different kinds of *guilt*, and for the sake of simplicity I will define two types in terms of my own understanding and relationship with them that I learned from one of my fabulous spiritual directors. I have had more than one over the years. Gretchen, college professor, clinical psychologist, and former Catholic nun, taught me there is true *guilt* and false *guilt*. I have passed on this concept to my own clients and have witnessed true transformation when *guilt* is no longer part of the equation.

True *guilt* is experienced if you have gone against your personal values and come to feel authentic remorse for your actions. This is an appropriate response after intentionally hurting someone and immediately regretting it.

False *guilt*, on the other hand, is based on that *should* baggage you carry in your back pocket. You have not defied your scruples, but you feel crappy. You haven't committed a crime or broken your moral code. You happen to believe that everyone else's happiness and well-being is your responsibility—a common belief among mothers. And this results in avoidance of your needs because you lack a sense of self-worth or have what I call "invisible" fear. This is fear of letting others down, and as a result, you let *yourself* down and get stuck in a pattern of circumventing your real desires. Taking responsibility for events which are out of your control is unproductive and detrimental.

This will sound harsh; get ready, and take a breath: Your fear of disappointing your child carries more weight than not attending a soccer practice or piano lesson. Your kiddos can learn from witnessing that you take care of what is important to you. Because when you honor what is important to you, they benefit by having a parent who has more energy and a fulfilled spirit. Will you strongly consider stopping using the *guilt*, the invisible fear, the elephant in the room to avoid acting on any personal wishes?

Examine your relationship with *guilt* and notice if it keeps you from taking care of your needs or if it's your constant spoken phrase when you do show up to yourself. Perhaps you don't create the art you love when your family is around because you feel *guilty* that there is something else in your life that you enjoy besides them. (Maybe at times more than them—it's okay, I won't tell.) You feel *guilty* doing things that don't involve your family and anticipate it will appear selfish. You think your time would be better spent doing housework because at least that will show visible signs of progress.

Is this false, self-imposed *guilt* truly serving you? Is anyone better off because of it?

REFILL REFLECTION:

- Watch your language—notice when you drop the "G" word.
- Check in with yourself. Evaluate this guilt.
- Consider what you now know and reframe your thought.
- Take ownership of your soul care without the "G."
- Fill your Cup.

SIP 25.

SQUIRREL

---

*"I'm going to meditate... wait, oh, I
see my book. Perhaps I will read
first... who left their shoes here?"*

Are you ever easily distracted, unable to focus on what is in front of you because a new shiny object has come into view?

When I'm acting like Dug from the animated film *Up*, my husband calls me Squirrel. Easily distracted, quick to pivot, wagging my tail like a dog, blindly pulled from one thing to the next.

Being easily distracted is part of who I am. Instead of putting a label on it, taking a pill for it, or figuring out if it's from childhood, having a lot on my plate, being an Aquarius, or part of menopause, I have found ways to work with it. Appointments are not missed; shit still gets done. I have practices I show up to again and again to keep my attention on what is in front of me.

Here's what helps me from chasing everything that makes my tail wag.

First thing each morning, I **get grounded to the new day**, the present moment, and my breath. Those few minutes of coming into the now clears away the cobwebs from my night's rest.

If I haven't **set an agenda** the night before, I get clear about what is happening that day, must happen that day, and I want to happen. I write it down. **Seeing the day's agenda helps me to remember my focus.** I use the whiteboard in the kitchen to write only today's schedule. This schedule includes appointments, commitments, and my fuel filling, as well as what is for dinner. One day at a time. Only the things that need my attention that day go on the board, and I wipe it clean for the next day.

As I continue with my day, if something jumps into my view like organizing the junk drawer or tending to an unfinished photo album, my brain says, *Oh, this needs attention, I'll do it now.* That can send me all over the place. What I must do next to stop the frenzy is **pause**.

The pause allows me to catch myself and ask: *Does this really need to happen now? Can it wait? Is this on today's agenda? Is this the best way to spend my time?*

When I come to the realization and clarity that this task doesn't need to happen now, can wait, is not on the agenda, and is not the best way to spend my time, it goes on my "for another day" list that I keep in my calendar. Although the unfinished photo album grabs my attention and sounds fun, realistically the time it will take will eat into my current agenda and send me up a tree. **I choose to stay on the ground.**

We can easily want to turn our attention to things that appear more appealing and entertaining. Come back to the moment and get clear on what your future self will thank you for doing today instead of tomorrow.

When the next shinny diversion comes my way, I remind myself what is up for today. Besides having my schedule or list to keep me on track, calling me back from distraction, I use the **twenty-minute rule**. I commit to doing something from my list, if it is a larger task for example, for twenty minutes. I **set a timer**. During that set time, I show up to the desired activity. As I notice my mind wanting to leave the room, activity, or task, I come back to the timer or clock. **I tap into my future self** and how she will feel when the twenty minutes are over. She will feel a sense of completion, pride, and satisfaction for sticking to the task and not getting pulled away. This sets me up for success as it invites me to align with one of my top values: accomplishment.

You will discover in the following "Sip" that **aligning with our values** has a plethora of rewards. Your future self has a better chance of showing up for your present self when tuned into your unique values.

A few more tips which help that I encourage you to try are to **write the words on your hand** that represent what your future self will feel at the end of your allotted focused time. Come back to the time, the feeling you will experience, and the task in front of you. It may take practice. **Add music if that helps.** As a **reward at the end** of your time, do something fun or perhaps something on the "for another day" list, like that photo album.

We've pondered how to be focused on important tasks and staying present. We can also get curious to determine whether we're avoiding our necessary refills by offering to help others. It's so much easier to look out for another. You were taught to do this, as I know there are role models in your life who have laid out this model for you. There is nothing wrong with helping others and even putting them first at times, but when it's done so your needs get shelved one more time, you might want to have a second look and ask yourself a hard question.

"What am I avoiding? What am I afraid of?"

Go on. Ask.

In her book *Daring Greatly*, professor, author, researcher, and all-around amazing motivator extraordinaire, Brené Brown invites us to ask for what we need and encourages this in her "Wholehearted Parenting Manifesto" as something our children will learn from us. If you want your children to take care of themselves and carry a full Cup, the first place they will learn this is from you.

Be the role model. Show your kiddos by allowing them to witness firsthand what it looks like to step courageously as you care for your needs. If caring for your needs feels uncomfortable, be uncomfortable. Through practice, the discomfort will lessen as the benefits appear.

Find the questions that work for you to steer you back. Make it simple by remembering less is more. We want to do fifty things in a day, but in reality, what we can accomplish will be a much smaller number. Choose an amount of time for your timer that makes sense to you. Most importantly, **be gentle with yourself** and understand how you're wired. New ways of being and habits begin with **one step**. One day at a time.

REFILL REFLECTION:

- If you are easily distracted and lose all sense of time or focus, use a simple daily list.
- Check things off, and don't add more to your list until you have plugged into yourself and determined if that task really needs to happen today.
- Use a timer.
- Tune in to how your future self will feel.
- Write the feelings or values of your future self on your hand.
- Fill your Cup.

DAY IS DONE
GONE THE SUN

———

When we ignore what matters to our
hearts, it catches up to us. We feel the hole.

I spent my thirties and the first part of my forties putting my head on the pillow each night feeling disappointed. *I forgot to call my friend. I didn't do yoga. I didn't read even one sentence of the book on my nightstand.* It wasn't the list of chores or parenting responsibilities, loads of unfolded laundry, filling out the permission slip, or paying a bill that I failed to attend to—it was a much more important list. It was the mental list of all the things I wanted to do, longed to do, and forgot to do **for me.** I didn't prioritize, stake my claim, or make space or time for me and I was mad at myself, disappointed I forgot, or frustrated there wasn't time.

As my clients started bringing up similar frustrations, I realized the problem. We rejected our values. **When something we value is not revered, a little hole is left in our well-being,** state of mind, and fulfillment of life. Rejecting our values may be unconscious at first. When we aren't honoring the substance our Cups crave because of lack of time, energy, or other resources we feel the hole that is created. It may get named as something else but I believe it is because our personal values are not given any light of day.

For me, I also let perfection of how I thought my time should be spent get in the way. I value connection, yet I put off calling a friend thinking there wouldn't be enough time for all there is to catch up on. I later learned a short call that begins with, "I have fifteen minutes to catch up, let's have a speed date," fulfills the connection to others I crave.

I want to meditate to give importance to the connection I receive from being quiet. I didn't have twenty or thirty minutes every morning, and I was too tired at night. This is when I discovered the power of a five-minute meditation. Connection, it turns out, is one of my number one values. As an introvert in an extrovert's body, it isn't always about connection to others. It is about connection to self. Then connection to Spirit. I was hitting the pillow not only disappointed but also disconnected from self. I ignored the five minutes that **nurtures my value of connection**.

Google "values" and you will be led to numerous resources that list core values and plain old values alphabetically. Start circling the ones that are important to you but you aren't currently making space for in your life.

That is the beginning to filling the hole.

Whether it's accomplishment, adventure, beauty, belonging, connection, community, solitude, or spirituality, get clear on what matters and write it down. This will kick off your awareness to the values that are of importance. **Scaling the value to a doable and meaningful amount of time** leads you to show up for it.

Often, you don't know the value of something until it is missing.

REFILL REFLECTION:

- Print out a list of values.
- Get a pen or highlighter.
- Circle or highlight twenty values that you forgot are important to you and you're presently not honoring.
    - If reflection is important to you and you are journaling for ten minutes every day and that is plenty for you, then you would not circle reflection on your value list.
- See if you can narrow down the list to five of the most important values to you right now in your life.
    - Pick one of the five.
    - Now, pick one action that feeds, nourishes, or honors that value.
    - Break down the action to something doable, pertinent, and achievable.
    - Put this action on an actual list, not a mental list, treat it like an appointment, and show up to it.
- Fill your Cup.

I BELIEVE IN YOU. DO YOU BELIEVE IN YOU?

You must believe first to see it.

Not a natural athlete and rather a natural optimist, my senior year of high school I tried out for the soccer team. I made the team. I'm not saying I had a lot of playing time but I certainly was right there on the sidelines cheering my teammates on, a participant in spirit if not on the field, and I couldn't have been happier.

Fast forward and I am that spirited mother on the sidelines of my daughter's soccer games. I'm that parent hollering out, "We believe in you; do you believe in you? Visualize. Create your opportunity." And my favorite, when the girls were in the fifth grade, "Find your inner Katniss." A reference, of course, to Jennifer Lawrence's character in the movie *The Hunger Games*.

This prompts me to wonder about you and your cheerleader or optimistic mindset—does it exist? If you naturally aren't the type to pick up your pom-poms or shout positive affirmations from the sidelines, stick with me. I may rub off. As a parent, I discovered my daughter's teammates quickly had a favorite cheer, and it was the one about believing, and this one stuck through their high school careers. They grasped rather quickly that for something to manifest, they had to first believe it was possible.

This is a great time to start taking note of your beliefs. A strong clue is to **notice what you say. Pay attention like you've never paid attention before** as you become a news reporter on what you are delivering as your truth. I'm talking about the everyday conversations you have with yourself and with others: *I don't have what it takes; I'm not good at that; I'm going to mess that up; she will be late; she will not want to talk to me;* or *I'm unlovable, unlikeable,* etc.

Sound familiar? **Your attitude is everything** on the field and in life. After you notice what you say a lot of, and particularly if you notice it is negative, ask yourself if you want a different truth.

Take what you say and flip it to what you desire to see for yourself: *I have what it takes; I'm learning how to be good at that; I'm supported;* and *I've got this; she will get there when she can; I'm grateful for meaningful connection; I'm rockstar beautiful, and I love myself warts-and-all; I'm loveable; I'm likeable,* etc. Even if you don't believe 100 percent in these reframed thoughts, you must decide what you want to see. When you are clear on what you want to see, then you can start believing the new vision. Believe it, see it before it happens, and then create it.

If teenage girls can inspire each other on the soccer field with one question—*I believe in you. Do you believe in you?*—then you can inspire yourself with changing your words. Plant the seed, pick up the pom-poms, and create the vision you desire. And I will ask you the same. *Do you believe in you?*

REFILL REFLECTION:

- What do you want to make happen? What are you ready to create in your life? Begin with shattering debilitating beliefs and replace them with positivity and possibility.
- Take out your journal and write down your beliefs. Beliefs about life, yourself, and others. Take an honest look at them.
  - Now, circle the ones that don't support you, that empty your Cup and keep you from moving forward in your life. Take one at a time and *rewrite* them in a new way that supports you, fuels you, and pushes you forward.
  - *Reframe* disempowering beliefs to empowering ones.
- Belief first, action second. We must plant our goals and dreams on fertilized soil.
- I believe in you and your goals and dreams, do you?
- Fill your Cup.

SIP 28.

PRACTICE, PRACTICE, PRACTICE

———

Practice is the best of all instructors.
—PUBLILIUS SYRUS

One of my clients was ready to quit smoking after thinking about it for an awfully long time. She began by changing out her morning habit. First thing every morning, instead of reaching for her lighter, she struck the yoga warrior pose. She had a desire to be a nonsmoker, and this led to her **commitment to replace something life-draining with something life-giving**. Doing this over and over, substituting one habit for another more than six years ago, turned into the story of how she quit smoking and has never looked back.

Muscle memory is a real thing. Dr. Wayne Dyer, the late motivational speaker, spiritual teacher, and author, wrote and spoke about saying "thank you" each morning when his feet hit the floor (Dyer 2017). This moved me to create my own morning gratitude practice. After more than a decade of whispering "thank you" each morning when my feet hit the floor, my morning gratitude practice is now my second skin. Without a reminder, I do so the minute I sit up in bed. His practice became mine. By doing it over and over, my body remembers, my heart is activated, and it has become a natural way of being, similar to putting the cap on the toothpaste after I put toothpaste on my toothbrush.

What second skin do you want to grow? What are you ready to practice, whether it's replacing an old habit with a different one or starting something completely new?

I desired to be a peaceful person. I wanted to be a person who meditated. I thought about meditating for ten years before I integrated this practice into my daily life. Now, after over fifteen years of practice, meditation is a daily habit that supports me. My journey began with five minutes and morphed into twenty minutes daily. The five minutes was my doorway and helped give birth to a longer and more consistent practice. I needed a gradual commitment to make it stick—now it's what I do without thinking about it.

Notice what you have been thinking about for ten years or much less. What do you think about doing regularly and don't take steps to do? Showing up over and over to a doable commitment builds the muscle not only of wanting to do it but also remembering to do it as it becomes part of you.

This also goes for a habit you want to break. Replace the thing you want to give up with the thing you want to integrate; substitute the thing no longer serving you with something life-giving. **The undoing of old ways begins with the practice of new ways.**

Beating yourself up with negativity won't be your ally in releasing old, non-serving habits. Play nice. **Replace talking shitty to yourself with talking supportively and positively to yourself.** Choose to show up as the winner of your own life. Actively show up to make habits that fuel you. When you decide to take on a new healthy way of being, or quit a life-draining one, there is something to be said for the process of repetition. When done again and again, little effort will be required, and your natural way of being will emerge to support you.

Think of the habits, good or bad, you have in your life. They became a part of your routine by continually showing up and doing said action. This action may have begun with a desire, something you repeatedly thought of for a period of time before you jumped in with both feet. This habit may have begun gradually, step-by-step, day by day. This is how you will start the new thing you are ready to incorporate into your life. If you find yourself frustrated, clinging to the old thing you wish to rid of completely, ask yourself, "What am I receiving by participating in this habit?"

Get honest with yourself, for in that genuine reality check you will **discover the truth to your choice**. The next question to ask yourself is, "What is it I'm not ready to let go of?" In your straightforward awareness will come that crack of light, which will help make the space needed for your change.

Do you need more questions? Tap into your reservoir of wealthy wisdom within by imagining you're asking a friend a question to investigate their own hanging on to something they want to stop. The **questions we ask others can easily be turned back on us** in a powerful way.

Yes, it's much easier to know how to fix other people's issues. I played this game for a long time. Now, when I am coaching a client and I offer them a suggestion that is applicable to me, I silently take note of it. As I turn that wisdom back on myself, I ask you to do the same the next time you are dolling out advice. When you hear yourself asking the person in front of you a question, pause and listen for *your* answer as it pertains to you.

Talk about light coming through the crack; get ready to blow the cracks wide open.

Strike a yoga pose.

"Thank you, thank you, thank you."

Your second skin will be easy to step into after you have done your new practice that first time.

REFILL REFLECTION:

- What is it you are ready to practice?
- Is there something you want to replace?
- Pay attention to what you want to do and are not doing.
- Write it down. Break it down to how often you desire to do this new thing.
- Once a day, once a week, or twice a month?
  - Be realistic. Then half that frequency and begin.
  - If you want to do something once a day every day, then start with three times a week.
- Practice that for a while until you are ready for more.

- Do this new thing over and over until it is your second skin.
- Be gentle and forgiving with yourself and ask those questions you would ask a friend.
- Go. Begin. Begin again. And again.
- Fill your Cup.

PART THREE

TOOL BELT

I can make a mean pot of soup. Before getting out the pot and turning on the stove, I must show up in the kitchen. I am the one to walk down the stairs to the backyard and cut the rosemary. I'm the one who pulls the knife out of the drawer to chop the garlic. Similarly, to me making the pot of soup means you are the one who shows up in your kitchen. Sleeves rolled up, hands open, and ready to get to work with the task before you. Personal growth and development can be hard work.

When a client has explained what it is they are struggling with, I invite them to roll up their sleeves.

"Let's play."

This is how I offer a tool that may seem heavy. We go slow, one step at a time. They try out the tool for themselves and let me know if it helped. If they need another approach, we make an adjustment, we tweak the tool, and try again. Or we pull out a new tool.

You can engage with the tools in this next section like it is your "play work." You have enough going on. Let's not make it a struggle. Let's take it lightly. Be gentle with yourself and, most importantly, be curious. Curiosity is an important part of change and evolution.

Everything you need is right in front of you. You need only to show up.

Utilizing the tools I offer in this section and throughout the book takes practice. You can have the sharpest, shiniest, snazziest tools, but you are the only one who can put them to use. Let's make this as simple as stepping out your back door to pick a handful of herbs for dinner.

STOP SPINNING

———

Ask yourself what you want when making a decision, and you will spin so fast you won't be capable of moving forward. Ask yourself what you need, instead, and an army of angels come out dancing, inviting you to listen for your answer within.

My life coaching clients often think or hope my job is to tell them what to do and to make decisions for them. Nope. I give clients the tools to make an informed, reliable, helpful decision without telling them which way to go. This happens to be one of the most popular topics clients want help with.

When it comes to the quick decision of what to do for the thirty minutes sans children, I offer "This or That."

"Should I go for a run?"

"Do I want to take a nap or go for a swim?"

For the big, critical life choices surrounding relationships, career moves, or to have a second child, I point clients toward their own inner bank of knowledge with a powerful discernment tool I have named "Choice A or Choice B."

"Is this the time to move across the country?"

"Should I leave my job?"

"Do I want to go back to school?"

"Is this the best time to get a second dog?"

These practices not only help clients, but they've also turned my world around, as I would much rather someone choose for me. Indecision leaves me with an even emptier Cup, agonizing over how to utilize an agenda-free amount of time or choosing between two different life-changing options. Head spinning comes from that game of tug-of-war that goes on in your brain—the place where fear shows up. Some of us are simply wired to be more decisive than others.

For those of you not naturally decisive with everyday choices or the big life-changing ones, I've got you covered. Let's address the fear and stop the head spinning as you learn tools of bringing every part of your being to the party, not only your mind. Are you ready to stop waffling back and forth and to be confident in your decision-making?

Okay, great. Listen up. This first decision-making tool stops the back and forth over the quick choice of how to use a short amount of time to your advantage.

THIS OR THAT:

- Ask a question that serves you well. Stop asking what you want as this starts the endless long list.
- If you aren't sure of the best serving question, try this: *What do I need?*
- A question that gets right to the heart of the matter— incorporating what you learned in "Sip 3"—*What type of refill must happen now: physical, mental, emotional, or spiritual?*
- Put your hands on your heart, over your gut, or on your hips in the Wonder Woman stance. These gestures invite you to tune in, listen deeply, and be empowered.
- Get still and listen.
- Allow the answer to surface.
- Count to three and get after it.
- Remember, it's a short amount of time. If you honor the first thing that comes to mind and you have the time, then you can go to the second action, the choice you didn't get to but also have time to include. Avoid the dilemma of "This or That" by going with the first one that calls your name.

When you take "want" out of the equation, you eliminate the long scrolling list that surfaces. Divorce your head and drop into your body, heart, and soul, as this helps you dive into what really must happen.

Now for the decisions that deserve more reflection and con- templation. Your head is part of the process and there are otherwise knowing, helpful parts of you that have so much juicy wisdom to share.

CHOOSING BETWEEN CHOICE A AND CHOICE B:
To make a decision, consult all parts of you. This involves connecting to your body, mind, heart, and spirit. If time allows, you can spend an entire day in contemplation with Choice A and another day with Choice B. A shorter amount of time works as well. Be sure to allow the same amount of time for your different options.

- **Get clear about your choices.** For simplicity, we will use two choices and label them A and B. This can also be used when the decision involves more than two choices. **Take note.** Get out a piece of paper and take notes, too. If possible, have someone record your answers or at the least write them down for yourself. Seeing your answers in writing will be helpful.
- Take a nice amount of time. If time allows, take an entire day. At a minimum, **take twenty minutes** for the entire process of deciding between two things.
- Begin this exercise by starting with Choice A. Imagine that you *have* already chosen Choice A as your final decision. In your mind's eye pretend this is what you have chosen. Sit quietly, knowing you are beginning with **Choice A**.
- Take three intentional deep breaths, allowing all parts of you to breathe in this first choice.
- **First, consult your body,** "How do you feel with Choice A?" Does your body feel light, heavy, energized, or exhausted? Know in your mind you are going with Choice A and consult all parts of your body. How do your neck and shoulders feel? Any tightness, discomfort, or pain? Tell your body, from head to toe, you are going with Choice A. What does your body have to

say about this? Your body has wisdom to share. Pay attention to all sensations. When consulting your body, experiencing a headache or fatigue knowing you're choosing Choice A is no accident. Feeling energized with an overall feeling of lightness is also no accident. Pay attention to what your body is saying, the pain experienced, and the energy—lagging or inspired.

- After consulting your body from head to toe, **secondly, consult your mind**. Your thoughtful, analytical, busy brain has something to say. You can pro and con it if you like, as long as you stay with Choice A.
- Interview your mind like you interviewed your body. What responses, facts, thoughts, and ideas come to mind? The mind has a tendency to future trip. Keep answers in the present moment as you have no control over what "might" happen.
- Now **consult your heart**. Place your hands over your heart. Take a deep breath and assess what feelings arise in your heart. Observe and be curious. The heart responds with images and emotion. Notice visuals. For example, do you see yourself as panicky or at peace? Excited or bummed you made this choice? Hopeful or confined? Notice the emotions. How do you feel about Choice A? What heart images are you receiving?
- After you have interviewed your body, mind, and heart, place your hands over your belly. Last and most definitely not least, it's time to **consult your spirit** and what some may call your gut knowing or intuition. This is that place of instinctive knowing, Divine wisdom. Undeniable enlightened perception comes from this part of you. You may ignore her much of the time, and when you truly are awake to her astute nature, she

doesn't let you down. She is highly qualified and delivers your truth. This intuitive place must be listened to as well as the other parts of you. Your knowing doesn't lie. Note spirit or intuition's response with your other observations so you can see it on paper.

- Time to rate Choice A on a scale of one to ten in regard to your **overall feeling of peace** with choosing this option. One = hardly any peace at all. Ten = full of peace, practically Zen.
- Now take **Choice B**. Do the **same process** as you did for Choice A. Don't skip this step, even if Choice A has you all excited and at peace with your decision.
- **Take a fresh breath, get up, and shake out your body.** Do the same process but this time with the knowledge you have chosen Choice B. Consult body, mind, heart, and spirit and then rate the level of peace on a scale of one to ten. Don't skip ahead.
- The layer beneath it all that we must pay attention to is our fundamental desire for peace. When you choose that which gives you the most peace when making a decision, you can breathe again, with no more paralysis and spinning ceased.
- Don't make the assumption to ignore the other choices when the first one feels right—see the process through to completion. If Choice A went easily and you came out of it energized, peaceful, and totally in your knowing, still interview Choice B. You may be surprised. Both sides of the coin must be examined—take good notes. Being open and willing and allowing yourself to experience both options is important, interviewing all possible choices before making your decision.

None of my clients regretted their choice made this way. The ones who ignored the answer that gave them the most peace, who ignored their gut knowing, were the ones who had regrets. You're **conditioned to make your decisions only utilizing your mind** and considering all parts of you is a whole new concept that takes practice. When you're interviewing your body, mind, heart, and spirit, the word *should* is absolutely not allowed. Many of us have highly developed *should* muscles, and it may come up when you consult your mind, but now you will develop new supportive muscles that will get stronger with practice.

Fear will want to creep in: hush it and don't allow it to take up so much space. Rely on the clarity you gained from utilizing the tools. Don't allow fear to cloud your enlightenment as you stay present. Nothing is more present than your body. It doesn't lie, and it has your back.

Fear is natural as it is your humanness showing up, but please don't allow it to steer your ship. Fear need not be your compass as you remember to pay attention to all parts of you. And if you didn't know, fear hangs out in your head. Drop back down into your body and listen to your inner wisdom. Cease the head spinning and game of tug-of-war. Trust the messages revealed and get out of your own way as you leap forward.

REFILL REFLECTION:

- Whether grappling with a quick choice of how to fill your Cup or a big decision, stop the head game and get clear using "This or That" or "Choice A or Choice B" tools to obtain solid footing.

- True discernment involves divorcing your head as the only leader and consulting all parts of you. Tune in.
- Fill your Cup.

SIP 30.

UNMOORED

———

When an untethered boat gets lost at sea, she
can always find shore with a good compass.

"I'm lost."

A new client said this in our first session.

"Do you want to be found?"

"Yes, please."

A recent divorce, job change, and move across the country
had my client spinning sideways. She no longer knew who
she was, as she had only identified as someone's spouse or
employee, and now she was standing in unfamiliar territory,
not only metaphorically but also physically. Naturally, she
was feeling uncertain about who she was and where she was
going. In that first session together, we defined her state as
being temporarily lost at sea. When you are lost at sea, finding
the shore can take some time. You want to believe the shore
exists, and you know deep down it does. You need to know

you will see it again. You're charting unfamiliar waters and completely stunned about how you got there, as it definitely was not a planned detour.

As my client and I dug around and explored the uncharted waters, she soon realized what was missing—she discovered what she needed. Her answer may surprise you, and I wonder if you can relate to the feeling of being untethered or lost at sea?

Have you been in the middle of change, temporarily derailed, uncertain of where you're going? Without belief in yourself, doubt, fear, confusion, and an overall lack of conviction of personal truth settles in and takes over. Can you name your missing anchor from another time in your life that kept you tethered?

When my client discovered what was missing, it was like a weight had been lifted from her shoulders as tears of relief flooded down her cheeks.

"I'm missing confidence. That is what I used to have, and with everything that has happened, I don't have it."

That's where we started. **This missing link would now become her compass.** She kept her eye on the shore, showing up anchored to being confident in her abilities, her truth, and the faith that this was only temporary. New life was waiting. By calling upon confidence, she found herself again. The time had come to tap into the strength and guidance confidence once gave her. Confidence was the guiding light that brought her to countless accomplishments and proud moments. The divorce, move, and job situation hadn't gotten her off track. She was off track because of her lack of belief in her abilities and her absence of courage and determination—her forgotten belief in herself.

Confidence was my client's missing anchor; can you name yours? You may have had an anchor pulled up from beneath you as you floated smoothly along the sea of life. An anchor may come in the form of a religion, relationship, job, belief system, or practice—one or all serving as the anchor that keeps you afloat. When life hands you new circumstances, it is an invitation to find a new anchor or resurface an old one that served you well.

When the religion hurts you, the relationship ends, the belief proves false, or the situation changes you feel as though you have nothing to stand on. The footing that once held you up is now absent. In these times, **it's about finding a new anchor, one that can't be taken from you**—like your breath, your meditation practice, or your beliefs—as it holds you up and brings you back to your center.

Being lost for a while is part of the process. If you're never stuck or lost you don't grow and evolve as these times wake you up, invite clarity, and invoke action. As yucky, messy, and scary as it is, being lost is vital—like springtime needs winter. You not only find yourself again but you also blossom.

My son told me when he was ten years old, "Mama, for every problem there is a solution."

He is right. For every time of being lost there is a time of being found. Without darkness there is no light. Recall your times of being lost. Did you make a new friend, find inspiration in an unlikely place, discover a new path, or reconnect to yourself? Recall that time of grace in your life when you got anchored after not knowing if you would ever find your way again. When you're standing in the middle of the mess, unglued, you forget you've survived being lost before, and that you will survive again.

THREE THINGS TO REMEMBER WHEN LOST AT SEA:
- You're not alone.
- You got this.
- All is well.

By tethering yourself to these beliefs, you already change your course and invite a new grounding. You open yourself up to a foundation of support by believing it is possible. **Your first friend on this adventure is yourself.** Stand in front of a mirror, say hello, and love the reflection staring back at you. Remind her that she can do this and she has done this before. Like my client found the confidence to guide her forward, you too will pull up your anchor and find your connecting link to lead you home one nautical mile at a time.

REFILL REFLECTION:

- Get in touch with what you're feeling and name it. Are you uprooted, overwhelmed, lost?
- Write it down and get clear about what it is you're feeling—no more ignoring, numbing, or shoving it away.
- Recognize what's missing so you can get anchored to something supportive and helpful.
- This might be what your soul needs right now. Allow.

- When the overwhelm or lost direction has served its time and you're ready to get found, make space to create your new compass.
- Ask out loud or in your heart, "What is my compass?"
- Will it be a word, a symbol from nature, a practice, a new relationship with self, or something else altogether?
- Get quiet and listen for the answer guiding you to what will best serve as your compass of truth, and then attach to it and hold on tight.
- Fill your Cup.

SIP 31.

OM

—

No one can tell you how to connect; you can only show up and practice, try things out, and be curious. If you're looking for the best way or to get it perfect, you will always be searching. Start. Where. You. Are. Now.

I'm not a meditation teacher. I don't even play one on TV. I do not have a license certifying me on the ancient art of meditation. I do, however, practice meditation and share my techniques with clients and retreat attendees. The best way for me to learn is by doing and fortunately I get lots of opportunities to grow and deepen my practice. You can read books on it, take a class, join a group, go on a ten-day retreat, and "learn" how to properly meditate, but if that leaves you putting off beginning your practice now, then please forget all that and start where you are.

Make your own rules as you play with what works. Explore the possibility as you pick up new techniques and methods. As I continue to learn, I find great reward in trying on different methods learned from workshops, meditation teachers, books, and friends but the **best teacher arrives when I simply show up and am present to the practice**.

HOW TO START YOUR MEDITATION PRACTICE:

Sit. Find a comfortable place to sit upright. Practice that first. Simply sit there. Place your feet on the ground. Rest your hands in your lap. Hand position isn't vital. They need only be comfortable. Try resting one hand on top of the other, palms up. If your space is quiet with minimal distractions that is optimal, but if finding the perfect quiet place keeps you from sitting, then sit where you can. Often, your parked car is the best place to seek solitude. Try sitting for one minute. If this is easy, add more time. If this is a pain in the ass and totally challenging, cool, make it thirty seconds. Thirty seconds is light-years ahead of not doing it at all. Cut yourself some slack. Only move on to the next step after you know you can sit for thirty seconds or more. Baby steps move mountains.

Be still. Once you have practiced sitting, now it's time to practice being still. Don't even worry about closing your eyes yet. You will get an itch. Scratch it. Many practitioners say to ignore it. I say scratch it. Remember, if this is your first dive into meditation, you are learning it from a girl who is wired like the Energizer Bunny on steroids, so I understand the nuance of not moving when you are a mover. Scratch, wiggle if needed, and only be as still as you can. Perfection is not the goal, so release it if it's blocking your progress. Get used to the idea of not moving. If you feel like a jackass, feel like a jackass, and do your darndest to do it without moving around a whole lot. Get quiet. Know you can't turn off your mind. Especially when you're focused on being still, as that's when the ideas come marching in.

Breathe. You have been doing it your whole life, this breathing thing. Please don't concern yourself with a proper cleansing breath, pranayama, or any other defined particular breath. Simply observe your breath moving in and out. Take in a conscious breath, hold it gently for a moment, and exhale. Let your breath come easily and naturally as you follow your breath with your awareness. When your mind hops on a thought, come back to your breath.

Focus. Once you are sitting still and breathing, you are ready for the next part. Decide if you want to have your eyes opened or closed. If you don't do well with your eyes closed, fix your gaze on a spot on the floor or near your feet that is roughly two inches in width. Allow your eyes to stay fixed on that area, blinking when necessary. With your head slightly bent down, keep your attention on that one spot. If you're able to stay focused like this, wonderful. Otherwise, close your eyes.

Note: If you fall asleep, cool. You needed to rest more than meditation. Let it be what it is. When your gaze is set or your eyes are closed, focus on your breath. Inhale. Exhale. Say *in* silently to yourself on your inhale, and as you exhale let only the word *out* cross your mind. That is your focus, *in* and *out*—those two words and your breath. When your mind wanders to the time, the laundry, the phone call, the vacation, or the conversation, gently come back to *in*, *out*, and your breath. Practice for one minute. You can set a timer, but don't worry about time right now. Only be present with your breath.

Let go. The thoughts are going to come. I get lots of my inspiration during meditation. You're finally stilling your mind so it may amp up. I invite you to put any thoughts on a cloud in your mind's eye and send them across the sky or put them on a boat down the river. You're acknowledging their presence and acknowledging you will tend to them later. My grocery list often shows up during meditation. Make a mental note to get eggs and put it on a rock in your mind's eye and let it roll away. Detach from doing it perfectly. Disengage from getting it right. Release expectation.

Allow. Be forgiving of yourself during this meditation practice. Allow yourself to do this even if it feels funny, doesn't seem like it's working, and is incredibly hard. Allow yourself to be uncomfortable. Allow yourself to practice. If emotion comes, give yourself permission to let the tears fall, the anger bubble, or the love pour out. Stuffing or numbing isn't necessary. Give yourself a hall pass as meditation figures you out. Allow the thoughts to come and go.

Listen. After you have a grasp of sitting, being still, your breath, focusing, surrendering, and you are allowing it all to unfold, it's time to listen. Spirit and Cup wisdom reside deep within. We're too busy, distracted, and noisy to always hear it. This is a carved-out moment in time to be still and quiet enough to hear. If nothing is arising, ask a simple question. If there is a particular area in your life that you struggle with bring it to this meditation place. Ask, "What do I need to know right now?" Then wait. Do your best to stay focused and come back to your breath. Wait some more. The answer may not come this time. Be open to receive when it does come. Your answer may come in a visual picture flashing before your eyes. A word, the face of a person, or a feeling may wash over you. These are all answers: receive them, be curious, ask again, and listen some more.

Note: Most meditation teachers will instruct that prayer and meditation are different from one another and that listening for answers is not a part of meditation practice. This is where I remind you I'm not a meditation teacher, but I am a life coach who has created a practice that empowers, enriches, and nourishes. I stand firm on the practice of quieting your mind as a great tool to discover your truth. Simply pay attention. The answers to your questions come in the stillness.

Be. This time of doing "nothing" is incredibly productive. You're so busy rushing around all the time that your body, mind, and soul need some time to catch up and connect. This time of being still and focused on your breath opens up blocked doorways and unlatches stuck windows. Relax into the power and gift of simply being.

That is one way to start meditation. You and your breath, sitting still, listening, and practicing as you continue to show up to yourself again and again.

REFILL REFLECTION:

- Are you ready to begin your meditation practice?
- Start one time a day for one week.
- Pick a short amount of time. No, one minute is not too short.
- Bring an accountability partner along for the ride. Ask a friend if you can report your progress to them.

- Put down the phone and the to-do list and become present to yourself.
- You can't mess this up.
- You're practicing being without doing.
- You're giving quiet a try.
- Fill your Cup.
- Your Cup will thank you.

SIP 32.

WALKING ON EGGSHELLS

———

*Holding your breath, waiting for
the other shoe to drop, is a slow
painful death to the soul.*

When I was a little girl growing up with my mentally ill father, I believed I had to put a smile on my face to avoid setting off my dad's mood. I would literally tiptoe down the hall as not to have anyone notice—not wanting to make waves. I carried that cautious stepping girl with me into parenting my own son, who came wired anxious and started showing signs as early as the age of two. Instead of being completely honest with him, out of fear of setting off his anxiety, I crept down the hall as I did in my youth—all in the name of keeping the peace.

Is passive behavior something you adopt to make life easier so that someone you love won't get their feathers ruffled?

Avoidance is cheating everyone out of growth, and it's far messier than a broken egg. I take complete ownership of my passive behavior, realizing when I'm not sincere in my communication with my son, I create a far bigger issue than anxiety. You come by your nature both from your **gene pool and your experience**.

Is your default response out of wanting to avoid discomfort and conflict? I get it. Perhaps there is a part of you that is a pleaser. Can you redirect your love and good intention down a different path? Would you like to cease tiptoeing and operate in another effective manner?

Pleasers want to keep the peace at all costs, right? Whether it's the exposure or eruption of feelings or anxiety you're trying to prevent, I totally understand the entangled web. The last thing you want is for your child to be angst ridden or to suffer in any way. The lesson I learned is that even though it's my job to keep my child safe, it's not my job to avoid real feelings and to tiptoe around truth, all to avoid what I assume will occur.

Of course, you don't want your child to suffer, and you protect them from pain because you don't want them to endure any more hardship in life than necessary. Here's another perspective: What if their anxiety, the thing you tiptoe around, is **part of their story**, their lesson which involves learning tools to squelch their fears and not avoid them? What if feeling the full expression of their emotion is integral to their development?

I know I wanted to protect my son, and this involved trying to avoid any anxious episode I assumed would show up. This always turned on me. He knew when I was dancing around the real issue or keeping him from something I believed would upset him. Here's something I created that has helped:

FACE IT:

- Flip your fear to love. Apply a loving feeling, word, or action over one based in fear. Exchange your notion of what you think could happen if your child feels anxious, or any other emotion you don't want them to feel, with a feeling of joy, peace, harmony, kindness, or any other emotion equated with love.
- Allow. Release any expectations. This includes expecting a repeat of past experiences or a projection of a possible future outcome. Get present.
- Courage. Give yourself space to take a breath and, before you respond with eggshell walking or pussyfooting avoidance, act courageously. Let your child know how you really feel. Let them know you are concerned with what you have to say and are worried about triggering certain emotions. Talk to them like they can handle the truth. Teach them that emotions don't define who they are but rather are guides that can support them. They will learn the value of an emotion from you. Teach them the value in all emotions, especially anxiety.
- Evaluate. Notice your energy and check your own trauma, drama, or fears to the curb. Your child can understand more with each passing season. Take an accurate assessment of what they are capable of by asking and not assuming.
- Integrate. Use your inner wisdom and ask your child for theirs. Yes, you are the parent, but remember, your child is also your teacher.
- Trust. Trust your kiddo. Trust they can handle their anxiety or emotions.

When you expect the worst that is often what shows up. Untangle yourself from any expectation. Act like they can handle it. This certainly gives more room for a favorable outcome than acting like they can't. Being completely honest with yourself and recognizing when you act out of fear—fear they will be uncomfortable, anxious, or get upset—is vital. See what can happen when you approach the situation with love. Getting through in a different way than last time or in a way you didn't know was possible is to witness a miracle. Leaning on the alternative to fear does that.

REFILL REFLECTION:

- The next time you notice you are about to walk into avoidance mode and tiptoe, *stop*.
- Take in a big fat breath and think about another way to proceed.
- Ask yourself, "How can I deliver my message and speak my truth without assuming, avoiding, or running away?"
- Be transparent. You can deliver your truth by being real.
- Fill your Cup.

SIP 33.

IN A WORD

————

Words are the Post-it Notes that anchor us.

My son and I have been each other's teacher in the anxiety department since he was nearly three years old, and he is now eighteen. For better or worse, our individual anxiety feeds the other. If he's worried or exhibiting anxious behavior, as his mom, I want to help, fix, support, and change his agitation. This rarely ends successfully, and it usually exponentially escalates the situation. If I choose wisely, his anxiety can be my invitation to take care of my own instead of adding to his. An invitation to keep my feet on the ground, understand what's happening within me, and face and embrace my concerns, and as I do so his anxiety drops down a notch. When I relax, he relaxes.

During the three years that I walked our son to the school bus, we needed something to get us from the front door of our home to the bus stop. We had visited doctors, psychologists, and naturopaths and tried vitamins, supplements, and every natural remedy you could think of, but he didn't want to go to school. He was fine when he got there; getting there was the hard work. He would worry about *everything*. Around this time, I was a couple of years into my meditation practice and decided to try something that worked well for me.

After my meditation ritual, I tune in to one word and invite that word to be my anchor for the day. I return to the word again and again if I am overwhelmed, anxious, or temporarily off track. Slowing down, plugging into the word, and breathing with it brings me back home to myself. I had tried everything else. I had nothing to lose by trying what worked for my stress and anxiety on my mini-me.

"How do you want to feel today, Buddy?"

"Calm."

After several weeks, my question changed. "What is your word today?"

By this time, he knew the drill and often picked two words.

"Strength and gratitude."

He would leave the house worried and fretting about the school day ahead. A block away from home, I would ask him to choose a word(s), and by the time we arrived at the bus stop the situation was hopeful. He was buoyed with confidence, ready to climb the bus stairs. At the end of the day, tucking him into bed, I would ask him how his anchor words helped.

"Did calm help you at school?"

"It was great. At recess, E was mean, and he took my ball. I got mad at first. Then I remembered to breathe *calm*."

"Then what happened?"

"E gave me the ball back."

On another night, I would ask, "How did strength and gratitude help you today?"

"Teacher M. was mad that I was taking so long walking back from lunch. I reminded myself that I am strong and was thankful for you and Dad."

For a few years of this anchoring practice, I began to record our daily words—his and mine. I compiled our words and chose the seventy most used between the two of us over a three-year period. This resulted in the Anchored Deck. My mindfulness card deck of seventy single words printed on the seven chakra colors has become a tool for my clients, retreat attendees, and others who resonate with one word, bringing them back to their center.

The fact that this useful tool was birthed out of a practice of necessity reminds me that our wisdom comes from within. Anxiety is a teacher and the word a tool to regain clarity.

**IF YOU ARE RELATING TO THIS, I HAVE
THREE INVITATIONS FOR YOU:**
1. Don't label your child's anxiety or your own, for that matter, as a bad thing.

2. Don't amplify their anxiety with your own.
3. Practice anchoring together with the tools below.

Getting anchored has not only helped my son and me but has also helped hundreds of my clients. Besides not being in the present moment, nothing can empty us more than our child's unhappiness and well-being. Am I right?

If your child struggles with anxiety, first take a breath. What I won't say to you is, "This will pass; it's only a phase." Although it very likely could be a phase, that doesn't help you or your child. Now, breathe again. Your breathing and your nonattachment to the situation will make a dramatic shift on their emotional state. If they don't sense your stressed-out temperament or fear of their anxiety being an issue, they have a much better chance of getting to calm.

GETTING ANCHORED FOR ADULTS:
- If meditation is already part of your routine, great, do this practice after your meditation.
- If you are not practicing meditation yet, this may substitute as your form of meditation.
- In the morning, have a clear understanding of what your day holds in store for you: appointments, commitments, responsibilities, etc.
- Pause long enough to take a deep breath. Hold your day's schedule in your head and the intention of who you want to be and how you want to feel in your heart with all you have going on, and ask, *What do I need today?*
- Be still. Allow the quiet to reveal your word as you hush your mind and breathe again.

- Let the word come to you like a loud whisper in a movie theater. You're tapping into your inner wisdom—let it emerge. With practice, the words arise more quickly.
- *Patience. Awareness. Calm. Surrender. Joy. Love.* Whatever it is, it's perfect. Don't question the word too much—let it be what it is.
- Write the word down. Trust the unfolding of its meaning in relationship to your day.
- Your job now is that at any time throughout the day when you're frustrated, stuck, or overwhelmed, recall your word. If it's not written down, you may not remember it right away. Tap back into the morning and your intention. Now get still like you did earlier in the day and breathe in your word. One way to do that is to turn it into a sentence. *I am patient. I am full of awareness. I am calm. I surrender. I choose joy. I am love. I give love. I receive love.* Or simply inhale and exhale your word slowly. You are getting anchored, and your word is supporting you.

The two versions aren't much different, but it's important for you to have an understanding and to use the tool yourself before introducing it to your child. Since energy is contagious, an anchored mama equals an anchored kiddo and vice versa.

GETTING ANCHORED FOR CHILDREN:
- Ask your kid one or both of the following questions after inviting them to take one or two breaths: *How do you want to feel today? What do you need today?*
- Let them come up with their word and, of course, if they need your assistance, ask if you can offer help.

Kids are far more creative and wiser than we are, so bite your lip and let them come up with their answer. Be patient, as this may take them a moment. And be surprised at how easy this is for them.

My daily anchor word grounds me to what I value most as I juggle all my tasks and responsibilities. My word brings me back to my breath, and when I get off track and allow the small bumps on my path to derail me, I become centered again—my intention of being *patient* or to *surrender* made clear.

Now, as a teenager, my son's anchor words help with a test, soccer game, or upcoming nerve-racking situation. Whether pulling him out of a spiral of anxiety or realigning my easily distracted mind, the difference comes in attaching to a life-giving word.

REFILL REFLECTION:

- Get still and breathe for a few inhales and exhales.
- Give yourself the gift of clearing your mind and ask yourself, "What do I need today?" Keep in mind how you want to feel, all you have planned for the day, and your intention of how you want to be through it all.
- Get in the practice of writing the word on your calendar, in your phone, or on a Post-it Note.
- Reflect at the end of the day on how the word guided you and helped you get back on course when your mind wanted to take you on a trip around the moon.

- Share this practice with your child, loved one, or friend. My son started at nine years old but definitely could have started sooner.
- Order my Anchored Deck—www.mamameedsarefill. com/get-anchored
- Fill your Cup.

SIP 34.

PINK DRESS

———

*In order for something to happen, you
first must feel it in your bones.*

The secret to manifesting your heartfelt desire is held in your
vision—see your desired outcome in your mind's eye, trust
it will happen, get out of the way, and allow it.

This is even possible while shopping with a teenager.

As a life coach, I support clients in manifesting their dreams.
As a student of life, I have been aware of the power of positive
thought being the gateway to those dreams manifesting. It
all begins with what you think and believing what you think
is possible.

Beyond thinking and believing it is also necessary to **feel like
what you desire is not only possible but that you already have
it**. You must let go of the details of how it will manifest, only
trust the unfolding. To think with faith means to think with
positive clarity and then let go, believing all is well. Meaning,
get the fuck out of your own way. (Did I say that out loud?)

Sometimes we don't want to manifest world peace, more time, or a loving partner. Sometimes we need a new dress.

As was the case eight years ago with my then thirteen-year-old daughter. Shopping is neither of our strong suits but a wedding was happening, and we both needed a new dress. With lots of obstacles against us—a loathing for shopping, a history of disagreeing about clothes, a short amount of time to shop, and a limited budget—we needed to be focused.

I had to **get rid of the old negative tape playing in my brain and replace it with a statement that held the power of possibility.** I had to release my limited thinking. I took out cash from the bank, to keep us within budget, before picking up my daughter after school.

"I say yes to finding an awesome outfit—dress and shoes—for my teen for $110 or less."

I believe that the Universe will deliver whatever it is we are aligned with, even material wants and needs. Is there something you believe you need or desperately want? It may not be a dress, but apply this method to change your mindset and get aligned with something you believe you need.

QUICK MANIFESTATION LESSON:
Figure out what you desire.

Be really clear.

State it to yourself and the Universe.

Ask.

Be open to receive.

Feel it happening.

Get out of the way.

Be grateful.

Believe.

My oldest child loved the mantra and even dropped the dollar amount to "$80 or less." We set out blasting Taylor Swift on the car radio. Three stores and lots of disappointments later, the manifestation was a success. Not only did we make budget with a dress and pair of shoes for my daughter, but I also found a dress I could wear to the wedding, not going a penny over our budget. We remained committed to our find, not knowing we would be hitting a huge sale. There was even a point where we almost gave up but chose to stay tethered to believing there was a dress out there.

Have you wanted something and almost given up at the first sign of defeat? That's when you must let go of controlling all the details. We didn't attach to where we bought her dress besides shopping at discount stores, and as we shopped, we stayed in gratitude. Gratitude can even be part of your mantra you create. *Thank you for the new dress.* You **must carry the energy of gratitude in your heart and act as if it's already delivered**—the Universe draws upon those vibrations you give the most attention. Whichever feeling is greater it will respond to, a reminder of like attracts like.

You bet you can create a vision board—a popular manifestation tool that works. My intention here is to offer getting in the right mindset and to see its vitality. A vision board will do nothing to obtain your dreams if you don't believe your dreams are possible. And here is another vital piece to manifestation: **feel the emotions you would feel when you have that thing in your possession**. Now, let's flesh out the quick lesson and give you some more guidance. For this example, let's use a parking space and being on time as the object of our manifestation.

Figure out what you desire: Come to an understanding of what you keep thinking about or hoping to have. You don't want to be late, so you believe a close parking spot for this crowded place will aid you in arriving on time.

Be really clear: More than a parking spot, you don't want to be late. Being late in your mind will cause lots of disastrous results.

State it to yourself and the Universe: I say yes to being on time.

Ask: I will arrive on time.

Be open to receive: I say yes to arriving on time.

Feel it happening: Being on time feels great. I am calm and focused as I get ready.

Get out of the way: Follow the traffic signals, don't break laws, and tell yourself, "All is well. I'm on time."

Be grateful: Thank you for all going smoothly, as I arrive on time. Thank you, thank you, thank you.

<u>Believe:</u> All is in Divine order; all is in Divine timing. Be at peace knowing you will get to where you are going in the Divine flow, safely and on time.

Holding this energy, don't be surprised when the parking spot is free in front of the building, the place you're going starts the event a few minutes late, or you arrive in perfect time. Instead of being surprised, be grateful. Say thank you to the Universe, traffic and parking gods, and anyone else you want to thank.

You aren't performing magic; you are calming down your mind and spirit and helping it to get to a receptive place to witness miracles. And even better than finding the perfect pink dress for your daughter or arriving on time to yoga before they lock the door, you are cocreating and aligning with all that is possible.

There is another element I'm leaving out but I believe to be vital when it comes to manifestation. I want to begin with baby steps if this is a brand-new concept for you. Know this: anyone can manifest something material. It's not rocket science. But the part I'm intentionally leaving out for now is that material goods don't fill us with joy permanently or provide spiritual fulfillment. Like I said, sometimes you simply need a new dress.

REFILL REFLECTION:

- Where in your life could a positive mantra shift your world?
- Are you tapping into the feelings that will go along with your desire?

- Be willing to create space for possibility with the words you speak, emotions you feel, and the thoughts you think.
- Fill your Cup.

SIP 35.

NOT THE WHOLE KITCHEN

---

*When my house is spotless, I'm
either getting ready for company or
avoiding the real work of living.*

"Procrastination is the most common manifestation of Resistance because it's the easiest to rationalize," author Steven Pressfield tells us in his book *The War of Art*. He continues, "We don't tell ourselves, 'I'm never going to write my symphony.' Instead we say, 'I am going to write my symphony; I'm just going to start tomorrow.'" (2002, 21).

Do you feel like that quote was written for you? Numerous times this has translated for me personally as, *I will take care of me after I clean the bathroom. I will make myself a cup of tea, read that book, or call a friend after the laundry is put away, the closet is organized, and the trash is taken out.* Of course, this is then translated to the laundry, closet, and trash being handled and my needs are forgotten. Then, the next day when that tea, book, or friend are still calling my name, I get out the vacuum. Sound familiar?

Would you like a simple system to help you deal with your household duties while not using them as excuses to get to the stuff that matters?

ONE THING:

- This is a flexible system in that it can apply to one room, one task, or one part of a larger task.
- Apply the power of *one* to your whole house or your entire week and allow the idea of one to be enough—to be whole and complete on its own.

One thing. *One part of the whole.* Let's say you are staring at a messy kitchen: a sink full of dishes, cluttered countertops, a dirty floor, and the list continues. Rather than dive in and spend an entire hour of undevoted cleaning attention, clean one counter. Wipe that counter free of dishes, crumbs, and visible chaos. Leave something on the counter that is aesthetically pleasing, something you care about: a cookie jar, scented candle, fruit bowl, or vase of flowers. Perhaps this is the counter you see when you first walk into the kitchen, and one glance at this organized space may drop your pulse and help you breathe easily. The rest of the kitchen can wait while you attend to your tea, book, or phone call.

Apply this principle to other rooms or chores trying to distract you from attending to your soul care. In your bedroom, making your bed first thing each morning sets the tone and makes an otherwise cluttered room appear tidy. Rather than washing all the dirty laundry, wash one load that is small enough to be folded and put away in the same day.

One thing. *This system applies to the whole house.* When it comes to cleaning, rather than cleaning your entire house on a Saturday, attend to one room a day as this creates order and structure while keeping time reserved for Cup-filling matters. Bathroom on Mondays, family room on Tuesdays, vacuuming on Fridays, etc. One room a day—one chore a day—spreading it out over the week takes care of the need for order and the balance of time. If it's not your scheduled day for that chore, leave it until it is. This helps take care of putting off your soul care because of housework. The cleaning will get handled on its appointed day.

I don't know about you but I would clean the bathroom every day as a way to put off that good book that wants to be read or that blog that wants to be written because it makes me feel useful and productive. I must remember that delegation is my friend, whether I delegate a task to a specific day or to another person. **Delegation will lighten your load.**

I can make housecleaning my entire focus, energy, day, and my entire life, and I know you can too, but let's not. Notice when you're cleaning **out of habit and postponing your joy.** Stop and direct your attention to what must be done.

Don't fool yourself into thinking a perfectly clean home makes a perfect mom who is worthy of staying home with your kiddos. Or that your chore will validate taking time for yourself. There will always be a chore. They never cease. This is your wake-up call to notice how much you put off for the sake of a tidy house. At the end of the day, crawl into bed knowing you honored the activities calling your name, and tomorrow you can do the chore assigned to the appropriate day and the second counter in the kitchen.

REFILL REFLECTION:

- What are some *One Thing* rules you can make for yourself that will support you in having some household order while not neglecting your Cup?
- What *One Thing* rule would eliminate procrastination and help keep your mind sane?
- Fill your Cup.

SPIN CYCLE

———

Meditation doesn't have to be sitting in the lotus position, chanting om for six hours. Meditation is about being connected and unattached.

I didn't want another load of smelly wet laundry. I plopped down on the laundry room floor even though it was time for me to go to bed. That's when I discovered that the spin cycle is under five minutes on our washing machine.

I imagine there are lots of tasks in your day that require a waiting period. Back in "Sip 13," and in other parts of this book, I have referenced waiting. Some of us are better at it than others. Whether it's waiting for water to boil, school to get out, soccer practice to end, or the laundry to finish spinning, is it true to say that much of your time is spent pacing back and forth for the next thing? This time separated out isn't long, but strung together, the minutes add up. Would you like to use that space of time between activities and responsibilities to fuel up rather than check another task off the list or scroll through social media?

Before you say *no*, remember that fuel must always be at the top of your list as fuel is what powers your Cup.

I am offering instead that you be mindful. **Mindfulness offers noticing without judgment and awareness without a measuring stick.** Being mindful is an act of kindness in its simplest form.

Constantly going, being on the move, and thinking until it hurts—your mind needs time to rest and recharge, and I'm not talking about sleeping at night. That night in the laundry room I had a choice to use those handful of minutes to get something done around the house, to watch TV, or to plug in and recharge. I was exhausted, and in the short amount of time I had to wait for a load of laundry to complete its cycle, I could've washed dishes, scrubbed a toilet, folded clean clothes, or ground coffee for the morning. I did none of those things.

Even though the laundry room is next to the family room I avoided flipping on the TV. I stayed in the laundry room, closed my eyes, and stood in front of the washing machine and sort of meditated. I was mindful to what I was feeling. I was quiet. I released judgment of "getting more done." I got still and aware and chose to be kind to myself.

As the washer spun the load of towels, I went to the place I go every morning in my meditation practice. I plugged into my happy place. I was surprised how quickly I got there, to my calm home within. I surrendered, standing amidst piles of clothes and the rattle and hum of the spin cycle.

You're conditioned to get shit done, to get it all done and then a little bit more. Little value is placed on **simply being**. I bet you put your value on what you can accomplish in a day. Not overlooking the incredible **value of being** is vital. Being present, being still, being in the room, taking up space, and simply being. When you stop doing, you give others silent permission to do the same. **In that stopping, you gather up energy, let the dust settle, catch your breath, and recalibrate.**

I almost laughed when the washer beeped, signaling the load was finished. I could have stayed that way longer, standing amongst the dirty clothes. I put the towels in the dryer and walked up the stairs calm, aligned, and centered. Five minutes earlier, I was harried, scattered, and tired. I was still tired, only now I was remembering to breathe with an intentional purpose. Grateful I found calm before going to bed. The laundry had finished spinning and so had I. Sleep came easily.

Do you often want to fill every moment with productivity? Do you have the belief that as a mother or woman being productive is part of your duty? Fuck that. I've learned stillness is incredibly productive. Maybe you can't visibly see the effect, but using time to wait to plug into yourself is priceless.

Even a short amount of time like those five minutes allows everything to recalibrate—your breath, your mind, and the constant busyness of life. You'll notice how much calmer you feel when you make this part of your practice. You'll sleep better, and you'll actually get more done when you leave breathing room between each task.

Your breath is opening you to replacing doing with **being mindful. Not mind-full.**

REFILL REFLECTION:

- Five minutes can seem like forever when you want to be doing something else and get to the next thing.
- Five minutes can be a gift of time to shift your thoughts and realign.
- Are there pockets of time, little moments you can rethink your actions and plug into mindfulness?
- Are you willing to receive a gift of time rather than fill it up with productivity?
- The next opportunity you have to wait for someone or for laundry to spin, how do you want to be as you wait?
- What if simply being was the most productive thing you could accomplish in that moment?
- Fill your Cup.

SIP 37.

THANK YOU VERY MUCH

—

Thank you is beyond good manners. It's the key that unlocks the bounty in your life.

"Thank you for everything turning out well."

"All is well, and I am grateful for the Divine unfolding."

"I appreciate this situation being resolved peacefully."

These are a few examples of how my prayers may unravel throughout the day. Instead of asking and hoping everything will turn out the *way I want it to*, I tune in to the possibility of things turning out even better than I could imagine. In the same vein, no matter what, I show up grateful. Grateful for what is and what will be.

What is your experience of prayer? What is your relationship with gratitude and expressing thanks? The two are interlinked in my mind as "thank you," no matter who it is spoken to, is an incredibly powerful prayer. "Thank you" not only acknowledges the person or circumstance in front of you, but it also opens the back door for something you might not have expected. Can I explain the science behind it? No. I can only share my experience. When I walk into a client session, family situation, or experience that makes me nervous with an open grateful heart, I'm supported.

Yes, of course I have been disappointed and experienced great sadness in my life, plenty of times, but what I know for certain is that with a **foundation of trusting and thankfulness, I am held. I am supported. I receive.** The Universe has my back.

Both my husband and I say "thank you" a lot. To each other, to our coworkers, friends, strangers, and children. We have never sat down and discussed this. It has simply become what we do. I believe it organically unfolded as two children of divorce, a mutual absence of strong reliable father role models in our lives, we chose to turn our sadness to gratefulness. I'm not saying this was intentional, but for our own reasons, we were the polite kids constantly offering thanks to those in our lives. My personality formed around not wanting another person to leave, hence wanting to be liked. I see the trail of giving thanks and link it to those years of cultivating politeness and clinging to being a pleaser.

When I wallowed in *"What about me?"* and what I get out of the deal, I was always disappointed. When I forgot to be thankful for what was in front of me, for life in general, it spiraled into one disappointment after the other. Choosing gratitude doesn't have to mean you are thankful in the moment for the heartache, calamity, or chaos. Choosing gratitude is an invitation to choose something in that moment that you do appreciate. Focus on something you view as good or simply recognize and honor.

Your story of gratitude may look vastly different, but I wonder if you can trace back your experience of saying thank you and notice the result of that expression?

For my husband and me, our thankfulness began innocently and grew into a habit. I didn't want to be abandoned, so I unconsciously believed being nice and polite would prevent this from happening. My husband is an incredibly and authentically grateful person, and I believe one contributing factor may be because, at a young age, his father left and never returned. Can I back this up? I don't know. I do know that whatever our reasons for saying thank you, grounding ourselves in gratitude blesses, grows, and works for us far more than stewing in what we don't have or didn't receive from our childhood.

Have you noticed the difference of approaching a task, the day, or your life with a thankful heart and how differently things unfold? There is a natural flow when the foundation is grounded in gratitude. After years of waking each morning with "thank you" on my heart as my eyes open to a new day, I'm cognizant of the effects of this attitude being kicked off on a positive note. When I'm not aligned with appreciation and gratitude, I have a rougher time. My crankiness runs the show and overwhelm and dread step into my viewfinder. There is also a practical side as it seems the appropriate thing to do. Saying thank you feels good.

Gratitude places you in the present moment, out of your head, out of worry and fear, and standing in honor and appreciation of what is in front of you. Thankful for the meal on your table, the friend holding your hand, the roof over your head, your breath, or the new day—an answer to a prayer even before the prayer is spoken or fulfilled. This spirt of fullhearted regard for all that is can help you refocus if you're only putting your attention on what's missing in your life.

From personal experience, gratitude helps me to nurture a **greater sense of well-being** and I'm not nearly as stressed out when I remember to step into gratefulness. I'm honestly happier when I am plugged into being thankful and appreciative.

You might want to speak up here and insert the question of how to be grateful when the hard, bad, difficult, crappy parts of life show up. Being in gratitude is not about wearing rose-colored glasses and only being grateful for the good stuff. When your friend calls to tell you about her cancer diagnosis or divorce and your own life is unraveling with heavy grief, being grateful for that news or loss in particular may not make sense, but on these occasions, it's helpful to find something to be grateful for.

Appreciation for a good doctor, lawyer, friend, therapist, or even for something not connected to the experience of loss— the blue sky, a comfortable bed, or a delicious apple. Turning attention to the abundance of life can bless the situation of grief and loss.

What you focus on multiplies—putting your attention on the sunshine in the middle of a storm can lift a cloud or two when you least expect it. Later, over time you may come to see the gift in the disappointment or heartache. Don't look for the lesson in the moment, it will reveal itself when necessary.

Being thankful in that place of waiting, that place of darkness, is like opening the window to let in the fresh air. Being thankful shifts the mood and turns things around. Back as a young girl my motivation to say thank you stemmed from wanting to be liked and included. Around the time of raising my own young children is when being a pleaser caught up with me, and I saw the depleting quality and the strong influence it had on emptying my Cup. Around that time, I also noticed the dramatic effect of gratitude. As a young girl, I may not have had the awareness that thankfulness was a way to attract goodness, provide emotional support, or lift me out of sadness, but as an adult I'm incredibly aware of the **link between my attitude and the outcome.**

Do you want a new relationship with gratitude? Begin simple. Every time you notice you are disappointed, ungrateful, or swimming in lack mentality, choose a different perception. I'm not saying don't be disappointed. I'm saying *also* find another thing to be appreciative of that may or may not be related to the disappointment. Keep noticing. In "Sip 36" we learned how to invite in mindfulness, now add a layer. After being mindful of your awareness, choose a life-giving thought or focus on another thing to be grateful for. **The things you give attention to expand.** Gratefulness repetition will build a new muscle. Over time, that new muscle will become more than a habit—it will turn into a way of being.

If being grateful doesn't come naturally, here are some ideas to get the juices flowing.

GRATITUDE PRACTICE IDEAS:

- At dinnertime, go around the table and say something you each are grateful for that happened that day.
- Gratitude jar: Keep a jar visible. Every day, write your gratitude on a slip of paper and add to the jar.
- Gratitude journal: Record one to ten things you are grateful for regularly.
- Each morning and evening, say out loud three things for which you are grateful.
- Ask a friend to be your gratitude partner, and text each other daily about the things that brought you joy that day.
- Send one letter a week to someone in your life who you want to thank for the lessons they have taught you, for the gift they are to you, or for your appreciation of them being in your life.

A regular practice of gratitude transforms to a natural way of being—it becomes a habit. You end up modeling it for others, rubbing off on them when your initial intention began with being aware of all there is to be grateful for. Begin simple; begin with thanks.

REFILL REFLECTION:

- Practice saying *thank you* every morning, first thing, to everything, and nothing in particular for the next five days.
- Make these two words part of your vocabulary. Thank the grocery store clerk for being there for you. Thank your spouse, your friend, your child, and the person staring back at you in the mirror.
- When the crappy stuff comes up, how can you focus on even one small thing to be grateful for?
- Start a gratitude practice.
- Fill your Cup.

SIP 38.

REPLACE WITH LOVE

———

The greatest of these is love.

—1 CORINTHIANS 13:13 (NEW INTERNATIONAL VERSION)

How does your partner, loved one, or someone you spend a lot of time with handle transition? Transition or change can set many of us off. Do you have your own moment of wigging out, whether internally or externally, when faced with change or transition? Often, in anticipation of something happening that we don't want to happen, we end up creating a much bigger dust storm. Remember this: **You have a choice** in how you acknowledge a situation. You have two choices: negative or positive.

Reacting might look like becoming defensive, angry, turning hostile, yelling, or acting in a way that adds more gasoline to the fire. **Responding might look like slowing down,** assessing the situation, taking a breath before speaking, dropping into compassion, removing judgment, lowering defenses, and being open. I don't know about you, but people in general, as well as life itself, give me opportunity after opportunity to make a choice in my response.

We are **constantly given the opportunity to react or respond.**

I have had lots of practice at reacting. I could blame it on being triggered by childhood trauma. I could pin it on having a sensitive child. I could make one excuse after another. For now, I will continue to practice with plugging into love.

When we choose to react to the fear, stress, or chaos of the moment, it's like turning on an amplifier. More of that will get created. When my son is stressed out and wrapped up in fear and I add my own fear and stress, we have an ugly hot mess. Vice versa when I'm upset and tied to worry and he plugs into peace, patience, calm, what is possible, and to love, the energy between us relaxes—**a miracle is born.**

Do you relate? Think of a time your child, partner, bestie, or someone you know well was stirring up the pot, having one of their moments, and that moment got bigger when you added in your own worry, stress, concern, frustration, anger, or fear. Use that example as a reminder of what can happen when negative and negative get thrown in together.

In those moments of big emotions, instead of being a magnet and adding in your equal or bigger negative emotions, pause. Consider the alternative of love. Acting with love, responding with love, and creating a new outcome. If you're demonstrating and giving love with your words, actions, and way of being, then the person in front of you will feel that and will likely get to the same place.

Be the bringer of change by responding like you want to, one breath at a time, patiently with practice. Write a new ending to the story of someone else's storm.

WAYS TO DROP INTO LOVE:

- Get in the present moment.
- Drop all conditions and judgment.
- Ask yourself what you would want and how you would want to be treated, and then give that to yourself.
- Ask the person what they need from you.
- Focus on what matters.
- Speak, act, and be loving—often that requires no words.

Stay committed to love. Let go of everything else: how it looks, how it feels, the fear, and the drama. Allow love to win by applying it again and again. If love is patient, kind, avoids keeping score, encourages truth, has hope, and seeks trust, how can you plug into it during those temporary moments of crazy?

REFILL REFLECTION:

- We are conditioned to react, but we are also conditioned to change.
  - What if you started the practice of responding with love instead of with the other hurtful, unhelpful, unnecessary ways you are conditioned to?
  - What are you willing to try?
- Fill your Cup.

SIP 39.

THEIRS, NOT MINE

——

What belongs to you isn't mine.

When I had foot surgery, my doctor told me it would be one year until full recovery. I responded, "Go big or go home."

I was having five different procedures done to one foot at one time. I was mentally prepared for this. I welcomed the idea of healing and the time I would need to allow for complete recovery.

"Are you off bed rest yet?"

"You're still not full weight bearing?"

"When did your doc say you would be walking again without the boot or crutches?"

All of these well-meaning questions from family and friends followed by daily texts:

"Wishing you a speedy recovery."

"Get better soon."

"Hope you are better today."

I have a caring family and attentive friends, and I am truly blessed with a community of thoughtful people around me. I appreciate them. My circle rocks. What I didn't realize is that subconsciously I was taking on their concern while working on keeping my own spirits positive and forward focused. Separating their fears and concerns from my positivity became hard for me. Their impatience from my patience. This translated to me being sad, frustrated, and annoyed, all the while not saying a word and holding their expectations as my own. This catapulted me to forget I was holding a positive healing outcome, and I ended up feeling like I was letting them down with my slow recovery.

"You're still in pain. Oh man, I'm sorry. I send you swift healing."

This thought of healing quickly was for their comfort and not mine. I wasn't about healing fast, but rather about a full recovery. I'm certain their "prayers of healing" came from a place of love, straight out of their big hearts, as they wanted to alleviate my pain and not have me suffer.

The thing is, I wasn't suffering. The surgery had resulted in physical pain and discomfort, not a death sentence. Their worry made me scratch my head and wonder if I was acting naive not to worry. I was holding a strange combination of my positivity and faith and their concern. Even with their thoughtful, totally loving words, the weight of their concern knocked me off-balance.

Another's opinion, perception, and concern doesn't have to be yours. Whether it's their belief that your healing should be speedy or their worry that something will go wrong for you, this all comes from their experience, their perception, and their hardwired ways of thinking. This is when it is important to **differentiate between yours and theirs.** Get clear if this thought has anything to do with you and if you want it to be yours. Remember the entire previous section on truth? If someone is interjecting their opinion, criticism, or worry, you get to stop and ask yourself, *Is this mine or theirs?* Instead of permitting their emotion to determine your feelings, detach.

What's theirs doesn't have to be yours. Other people's worry or even their joy is none of your business. I will say it again: it's theirs, not yours. Their opinion stems from their experience, and they are projecting it onto you.

You may be wired similarly to me and automatically and unconsciously take on others' feelings and allow their concerns to be yours. Practice letting that go by reminding yourself, *Theirs, not mine.* If you're wanting to comfort them, comfort yourself instead. After you give yourself the comfort, care, and attention you need, perhaps a loving boundary can be set in place. Being in gratitude for having someone love you enough to be worried for you is a gift, even though it is an uncomfortable one. Be gracious and willing to state what you need.

A tool that helps me and my clients when a boundary is needed is to **visualize a wall of protection** all around me so I am not breathing in other's emotions. I have fun with my imaginary clear umbrella. I think of it as a loving armor of preservation.

The only thing that can get in is light. Everything else bounces off my giant bubble-shaped umbrella. Try it. This visualization allows you to **release any ownership** of other's opinions, thoughts, worries, or discomfort.

Let's be honest. No one likes to see anyone suffer. This is the spark that ignites another's concern for you. The assumption that your physical pain is causing you suffering weighs a ton of bricks. This brings us back to "Sip 17" and assumption-making. Clear up any assumptions or put up your umbrella.

After you remember to breathe, open your heart to gratitude, and safeguard yourself with your imaginary armor, let go. Their worry is theirs, and you need not take it on as your own. Any assumptions of your pain, frustration, or experience are theirs to own as well. You don't have to agree or take any of it on. Rather, you get to feel blessed for having people who care so much about you. Then, get back to recognizing and honoring what is yours.

REFILL REFLECTION:

- Where in your life are you being invited to release another's thoughts, opinions, good wishes, and ideas from your own?
- Where can you detach?
- Tap into your truth.
- Fill your Cup.

WALL OF FLOWERS

———

Cover up so only the light can get through.

"I want to stop volunteering in my son's classroom; this woman drives me crazy."

My client was having a hard time with another parent. The volunteer hours at her child's school were becoming something she dreaded because of the energy of this other mom. My client was feeling belittled, bothered, and emotionally bruised every Tuesday afternoon at her son's school.

"Let's try something," I offered.

I invited her to close her eyes and **imagine a place where she experienced feeling peaceful and protected.** Her place of safety and tranquility was a garden full of peonies, poppies, dahlias, delphiniums, and roses of every color. I assigned her the task of imagining a wall of flowers surrounding her every Tuesday when she volunteered in her son's classroom.

Being an artist, she drew a self-portrait of herself surrounded by flowers every color of the rainbow. She tucked the picture in her wallet, and on her first Tuesday, armored with her imaginary protective petals, she had a lighter step down the elementary school hallway.

"You'll never believe it," she excitedly reported on our next call. "The mom wasn't annoying yesterday."

"Tell me more."

"I parked the car a few minutes early like you suggested and imagined my wall of flowers. Full of beauty. The only thing that could get through was sunlight. Exactly like you suggested. She stayed in her own space and said very little to me. I was able to leave the school feeling recharged unlike other Tuesdays for months."

Clients have imagined a clear umbrella, a shield made of their favorite color, a forest of bamboo, a giant red heart, and many other creative visual barriers of protection.

This client, six years later, still reports how that simple imagery altered her experience of another's energy. She now uses it with her teenage son. Sure, she is frustrated when he doesn't talk to her or chooses to yell at her for no apparent reason. Instead of allowing his anger to be hers, her wall of flowers reminds her of her truth and **keeps her centered**.

You can pick up others' energy all day long as I mentioned in "Sip 21." It sounds so simple and a bit *Pollyanna*, but **what you see in your mind's eye matters**. What if you picked a protective imaginary layer and stepped into it before seeing that challenging relative, coworker, or acquaintance. Your mind is more powerful than you realize. Your mind has the power to repel negative interactions and hold off another's apathy, anger, and attitude becoming your own.

REFILL REFLECTION:

- Come up with your own imaginary armor of protection.
- See yourself being wrapped up in it while in an uncomfortable situation.
- Put it on daily when you brush your teeth.
- Use a visual cue to remember.
- Fill your Cup.

RASPBERRY MEMORIES

———

*A touch, a smell, a taste, a sound, or
the sight of the slightest hint of joy can
shift a mood from winter to spring.*

Apple pie. Peppermint tea. Vanilla scented candles. Rosemary from the garden. Chocolate chip cookies fresh out of the oven. Roasted garlic. Rain.

Do you have particular smells that catapult you back to a happy memory of your childhood? Or do you think of your Aunt Frieda every time you see someone wearing rain boots? When your senses are triggered, you can be transported to a time in the past in the blink of an eye.

What do you think of when you smell or taste raspberries? For me, I am back in 1973 picking berries in my grandma's yard. Then eating a bowl of raspberries covered in cream and sugar at her kitchen table. I can be mad, sad, or in a funk, and the slightest whiff of raspberries removes all angst from my mind as I feel her standing in the room with me.

Is your mood altered when you drink a mug of Earl Grey tea, light a lavender candle, or wash your hair with mango-scented shampoo? Your senses are so connected to your attitude and mood that it's no wonder there is such a thing as addiction. But let's look at this as a positive, rather than creating a drug habit.

When our son was little, lavender-scented oil would help him fall asleep and wild orange-scented oil picked up his spirits when he was worried about a test at school or attending a social gathering. I can report the same kind of favorable result from dabbing essential oils behind my ear or at my heart chakra. Smells are so powerful. **They transport, comfort, remind, and heal us.**

Do you perk up and have an attitude shift from the smell of coffee, cleaning products, or a particular food cooking on the stove? Start to notice what smells, tastes, touches, sounds, and sights affect you positively. Keep this information in your back pocket. When you're aware of a need to buoy your spirits or shift away from negativity, know what sights, sounds, smells, tastes, and touches can help you. A drive to the mountains, the sound of the ocean, the smell of grapefruit, a mouthful of apple pie, or gently rubbing your head may all be the simple refill to put you closer to full.

It sounds so simple; all the more reason to try it. A slice of lemon in your water may assist you in drinking your sixty-four daily ounces, and a good song may boost your attitude during the bewitching hour as you figure out what to make for dinner. Blasting the Rolling Stones or Barenaked Ladies with the wind in your hair cruising down the highway may be the ticket your soul craves. The **little things in life bring you joy.** The little things get you from empty to full.

REFILL REFLECTION:

- Make a list of your favorite sights, sounds, smells, tastes, and touches, and know how to access them in a pinch.
- Whether you keep a tea bag in your purse or have a musical playlist on your phone, know how to refill by tapping into the sense needing your attention the most.
- Fill your Cup.

SIP 42.

TICKET FOR ONE, PLEASE

————

A vacation is a state of mind.

"They're like a day spa for your soul," says Amy Anderson, a regular attendee of my sack-lunch-mini-retreat that I have been holding since 2010 (Silver 2016).

She drives across town and attends my four-and-a-half-hour day retreat and drives home restored. Vacations and retreats are a wonderful recharge. But they're not always possible. Sometimes, you can't wait until you have the time or money saved up and space in your schedule to take off a week from work to fly to an exotic location for restoration and rejuvenation. That was my motivation for creating something simple, local, and short.

My friend Erika and I walked one morning a week when our kids were in grade school. We happen to live in a wonderful part of Seattle where we need only walk a couple of blocks, and we can see the Olympic Mountains and Puget Sound. On one weekday morning, when I showed up on her doorstep, it had been two weeks since we last walked together.

Skipping our usual hugs and greetings, we both got right to the point, "Time for a long one today?"

Reading each other's minds, we were both in need of and had time for a long walk, which meant one thing: We were headed to the beach. I even had a ball in my pocket to throw for my dog, Buford, so he could swim. Most vacations call for a swim, right? His tail beat wildly with anticipation. We headed down the hill, catching up on the last two weeks. Children, work, her art, my writing, husbands, recipes, hope, and longing, breathing easily among the comfort of trees and each other's company.

We listened deeply and laughed hard as we swapped stories. Taking in the beauty of the Olympic Mountains and Puget Sound, we heard the seals barking and gulls squawking. An hour later, after we had caught up, Buford had a chance to swim, and we had broken a sweat coming up the big hill, Erika says to me, "Ah, it's like we had a vacation."

Two blocks from her front door, I looked over at Erika, seeing the mountains and water behind her and my dog wagging his tail between us, and smiled.

"Totally. You nailed it. And it's not even ten in the morning."

Vacation is a time to **rejuvenate**. A stretch of time when you let go of responsibilities and gain new strength. Good weather is often involved, and surrender is indeed a necessity.

Laughter and good company are both an added bonus. I was completely recharged from our morning spent among trees and walking near water.

When you are on vacation, you let go of responsibilities, relax, go with the flow, and leave the worries and stress of everyday living behind. **So why do we wait and only do this once a year or once in a while?** What if we took on a new perspective and adopted another version of a vacation? I am proposing one without the expense, waiting for vacation hours to accumulate, or getting a dogsitter. We can keep our vacation needs in check in between our getaway opportunities by taking advantage of our own environment.

Erika and Amy's comments are the essence of a Mama Needs a Refill sack-lunch-mini-retreat and the concept behind retreating, going within, turning off the noise in our heads, and plugging into ourselves. An authentic recharge awaits. It doesn't have to be a vacation with the family to Hawaii or a yoga retreat by yourself in Taos. **A vacation can be stepping outside of your usual or simply stepping outside.** Allowing yourself to let go and receive. For me, a retreat *is* a vacation. You are **going within, turning off the noise, and turning inward**.

The Merriam-Webster dictionary defines **"retreat" as an act of withdrawing**, a place of privacy, or a period of group withdrawal for prayer, meditation, study, or instruction under a director. What if we made this a regular practice and you were the director? What if we made it even easier than my mini-retreat and we set you up to create your own version of a mini-vacation regularly?

As we have all heard the phrase, it's about the journey, not the destination. Every Wednesday morning for three years Erika and I took a vacation. A short journey only a couple of miles from our neighborhood. The flight took off at 8 a.m. when I arrived on her front porch. No baggage to check, no passport to update, travel agent unnecessary, and no need to call in sick. This vacation with a friend provided companionship, laughter, unexpected adventure, exercise, and soul-filling connection, and it didn't keep me from my day job and responsibilities. The short excursion enhanced my engagement with my everyday tasks and added sunshine to my day without needing sunblock or dealing with jet lag.

After my fortieth birthday four-day celebration on the Oregon Coast, a seed was planted to create something with a realistic timeframe that worked with busy schedules. With less than five hours during the day when the kids are in school, taking a half day off work during the week was the solution to filling the need to unplug without waiting for the next planned vacation.

You don't always give yourself space to consider your wants, desires, and needs. You're needed from the start of the day until you put your head on the pillow at night. In between those hours, from start to finish your energy is spread thin as your time, creativity, actions, and awareness is spent toward everyone else. Juggling the individual needs of each child, not to mention their relationships with friends and teachers requiring your planning, coordinating, and negotiation efforts.

At the end of a day, there is no more time to turn within, and all you can do is drop your head on the pillow to wake up and do it all over again. When others need you, turning your attention to them primarily becomes habit and leaves no time or space to consider your own needs and concerns.

Over and over women leave the mini-retreat recharged with having time all for themselves and a **new appreciation of what it means to honor their needs.** What about you? Could you use a mini-retreat? I will lay out an outline you can follow or use as inspiration for your own creation. Remember, getting your nails done or hair trimmed and foiled is not a mini-retreat. Maybe those appointments can be your weekly vacation. This experience is about going within so you can emerge with more to give. And even more, so you can give without wanting to run away.

In the silence, we hear our own wisdom and the calling out of our Cup. To unplug from the demands of your life means to plug into the calling of your soul and it's vital to your physical, mental, emotional, and spiritual well-being. You're not the only one fed by that nourishment. Everyone in your circle feels the effects that time, space, and energy give to your Cup.

YOUR MINI-RETREAT:
- Plan to get out of your house.
  - Go to a park, the beach, or anyplace you're not distracted or drawn to carry out your usual responsibilities.
- Pack some essentials: food, water, a book, a journal, a pen, and music.
- Intention is everything. Set an intention for your time. (*To be recharged, to discover something new about yourself, to relax, to gain clarity.*)

- Plan activities for these four areas of refilling: physical, mental, emotional, and spiritual.
  - Physical: walk, yoga, run, swim, dance—moving your body in a way that feels good.
  - Mental: reading material, coloring, art project, or take a nap.
  - Emotional: journal to get in touch with your feelings, use any of the refill questions in this book to find clarity.
  - Spiritual: connect by prayer, meditation, stillness, or being in communion with nature.
- Have closure to your time with a ritual that makes sense to you. (See "Sip 9" for ritual ideas.)
  - Ask yourself what you are now committed to after this refill time and create a piece of accountability. (Once a day breathing or daily gratitude, for example.)
  - Write that accountability in your calendar. Tell a friend or partner and show up to self.

At one mini-retreat covering the topic of mindfulness, Ester, mother of four, working full-time outside of the home, discovered a newfound connection to self in the short time. "This is the first time I've had more than a few minutes to think about my needs."

Taking that time can be the spark to light your fire of soul care. It is essential to check in, plug in, and receive.

The wonderful thing is you don't have to hang on to your empty Cup until you can afford and plan a long vacation. When you **give yourself permission and allow** yourself this time and space of personal connection, the honoring of your whole self will be evident to those in your life. Your calmer aligned state will ripple out into all your interactions. If you aren't ready to give yourself four hours, start with one and call it a mini-vacation. When you're ready to retreat, it will require a wholehearted commitment to be renewed for the greater good of all. Four hours is nothing, and four hours is everything.

REFILL REFLECTION:

- Plan to get out of your house.
  - Ask yourself what you value and yet don't make time for.
  - List out the things that would make you smile, warm your heart, or light you up.
  - Who would you want to bring with you? Where will you go? What will you do? The world around you is full of opportunities.
  - Start with thirty minutes. Put the activity on the calendar and strap on your favorite shoes.

And of course, to be clear, shoes are totally optional.

- Ready for something more?
  - Plan your own mini-retreat, either alone or with friends.
  - Use the outline from *Your Mini-Retreat* above.
  - At the very least, plan a chunk of time with your phone turned off as you do activities that draw you inward.
  - Integrate silence, music, nature, movement, and other activities you don't normally partake in but, you know, fill your Cup.
  - What aspects of this time design do you want to explore only for you?
- Fill your Cup.

PART FOUR

TEACHER

When I played "school" as a girl with my childhood best friend Jill, I always wanted to be the teacher. As a teen, I taught Sunday school in church, and after college, I went on to be an English teacher in Japan. Later my children became my students. I found myself teaching life coach certification, writing groups, and leading circles of women to fill their Cup and find their voice. As much as I enjoy sharing tools and offering guidance, I want to always remain a student.

A student of life. There is so much to learn. So much to unearth about myself and about this world. The minute I let go of believing I have all the answers, the more I learn.

When I took the chip off my shoulder, thinking I already knew all I needed to know, I had the most exciting revelation: Everyone in front of me is my teacher. Regardless of if it is the person or the interaction, I believe life is constantly handing me opportunities to grow. To absorb and assimilate.

One of my favorite parts of being a mom to our two kiddos is how much I learn from them. I'm not talking about how to pose for a BeReal photo or do the latest TikTok dance, although these are fun. My children are my teachers of how to live. My teachers of how to love. No longer pretending in front of a childhood classroom with my best friend but living deeply. Looking at the bruises and honoring the lesson.

The world is our teacher. Teaching us to understand ourselves better; teaching us exactly what we need to know, let go of, and embrace.

My favorite teachers are the unexpected ones. The hard lessons. The parent-fail. The stranger in front of me at the grocery store igniting my triggers or offering a hand. Getting off a client call and realizing I got paid to learn my own lesson, to coach myself. The, "Oh, I get it now why that bothered me so much," lessons. The ones in front of me, every damn day.

Oh, Life, thanks for teaching me.

WISDOM OF THE CIRCLE

———

*Life is a circle, and we must
remember to look around it.*

By the look on my face, my husband knew it wasn't a question.

"I'm thinking about signing up for a weeklong writing retreat."

Our son was almost three years old, and I rarely got away from our children, when an amazing opportunity presented itself. At this point, I was staying at home with our children full-time and only fantasized about stepping away. When an opportunity arose to attend a weeklong writing retreat, I saved my pennies, called on friends, and told my husband he needed to take time off work.

Driving to Whidbey Island, not a very long distance from our Seattle home, I was flooded with emotion, thoughts, fear, and doubt.

Would everyone be okay at home? Would I actually get writing done? Was it ridiculous to be doing this? I'm not even that good of a writer.

And honestly, the excitement outweighed all the other stuff. *I was getting away. I was doing something I had been wanting to do for a long time.*

The first thirty minutes of my arrival I explored the grounds of Aldermarsh like a kid let out of detention. I breathed in the mint growing abundantly in the organic garden. I spied a fox in the woods. I touched the long grass that boarded the property. I found a spot in the sunshine and drank in the voiceless seclusion like it was the bottom of a 7-Eleven Slurpee. When your companions are under the age of five, sucking up all the simple goodness nature can offer is a welcome balm to the spirit. All of a sudden, a ladybug is a magical creature you have never before encountered. The sound of bees, hummingbirds, and rustling leaves all a welcome buzz, an invitation.

On day three of the writing retreat, our fearless leader, Christina Baldwin, founder of PeerSpirit Inc., shared with us the significance of sitting in a circle. We gathered each morning and evening in a beautiful building that had floor-to-ceiling windows looking out on the tall grass and expansive gardens. Occasionally, a deer or two would saunter by the window while we were sharing about our writing focus, offering patience in their calm curiosity.

Apparently, when you are gathered in a circle, **the person on your left is your warrior, the person on your right your healer, and the person directly in front of you your teacher, leaving us each as the visionary**. I learned the circle practices Baldwin taught for decades that week and use them to this day in my own retreats.

We all have something to offer and teach. All of those around us in a deliberately seated circle or beside us in line at the bank have the potential to inspire, educate, enlighten, and lead us to a personal truth or teach us about something we've always wondered about.

That week, the woman on my left was my warrior as I later discovered her story of losing her partner. My lesson in compassion. I was her healer as I shared my experience of being raised by a mentally ill father. The woman in front of me, without even knowing it or doing anything on purpose, invited me to take risks. Her story became my inspiration, and her experience linked me to my own healing and self-discovery.

That is how it can be. Sitting quietly in a garden and the creature out of the corner of your eye can offer an answer to your long-wondered question. A stranger can share their heartbreak, and you find healing for an old wound.

We need each other. Not only to be one another's warrior, healer, teacher, or visionary but also to pull out the hero in all of us.

REFILL REFLECTION:

- The next time you are in a circle, notice who is around you.
  - Pay attention to what they share and how their words, story, or experience can contribute to yours.
- The next time someone in front of you is annoying you, be still and listen. How is what they are doing or sharing your lesson?
- Fill your Cup.

SIP 44.

ASK AND OFFER

———

Giving and receiving are two
polarities that need each other.

Did you know that when you say *yes* when someone gives you a gift or offers you their help, you're giving them a gift back?

I have often been more comfortable with giving than receiving. Are you the same? Have you become so accustomed to giving your attention, time, and energy that you don't even know how to receive? When we can receive with open arms, everything shifts—the bitterness, the struggle, and the imbalance.

When a dear friend offers you a break, a piece of chocolate, a hug, or a gift of love and support to help you, and you give them your conditioned response of, "No, thanks," that implies, "That's okay, no worries. I don't need the kindness you are offering." You are shutting down the natural flow of giving and receiving. You're so uncomfortable with receiving that you have lost any awareness that **every giver needs a receiver**. As predictable as it is to turn down help, do you realize that when you say *no* to receiving an offer of assistance or a gift in any form, you're shutting down someone else's giving?

You're actually giving to another by saying *yes* to their offer. You're empowering them by receiving, and you're keeping the natural flow alive. That is how much we need one another. Receiving doesn't come as naturally as giving. I get it. You feel good when you give and needy, desperate, unworthy, uncomfortable, and incapable when you receive. Look at it this way: As you accept someone's gift or offering, you're providing them with satisfaction and purpose. Read that line again. As you accept someone's gift or offering, you're providing them with satisfaction and purpose. Don't make me say it a third time.

Henri Nouwen says, "Receiving […] means allowing the other to become part of our lives. It means daring to become dependent on the other. […] Receiving with the heart is therefore a gesture of humility and love" (Henri Nouwen Society 2018). Giving may come more naturally, but **both polarities of giving and receiving thrive with the other**. The opposites require one another. **Every giver needs a receiver like every receiver needs a giver**.

Do you struggle in the receiving department? Perhaps you always say, "No, thanks," or, "I got it," and prefer to do it all on your own. There is no secret formula to receiving but I do have some tricks and thoughts up my sleeve I would be delighted to share with you, so you can get more comfortable and eventually not turn away another offering that comes your way.

First, get clear to the reason behind your challenge with being the receiver. Do you feel like you are being a nuisance or are providing hardship to the giver? Do you feel unworthy or awkward in the spotlight? Come back to the repeated phrase above and let it sink into your bones that **receiving is another way of giving**. You're giving so much in your acceptance from the giver. You're not being a nuisance. They're offering help, and if it were a hardship, they wouldn't offer. Next, it may take a lifetime to learn your worthiness so trust me on this, again, they wouldn't offer if they didn't see you as worthy. And if it's the spotlight you have a challenge with then know you are making a bigger deal and drawing more attention by saying *no* so you might as well say *yes*.

Christina Baldwin, the author of *The Seven Whispers: Listening to the Voice of Spirit* and one of my mentors and Circle facilitators, has helped me to have a different awareness around this. One of her tenants she invites the reader to practice is **asking for what you need and offering what you can**.

Her words of wisdom speak right to my heart and open up a window of grace making the **act of receiving feel powerful rather than burdensome**. When I do that very thing of asking for what I need and offering what I truly can, a better version of me comes to the table. I can honor the giver I am while not depleting my Cup. And I can look at receiving as another avenue toward giving, allowing someone else to be the giver.

When you start off saying *yes* to not disappoint, you are creating inauthenticity, a definite Cup drainer. If you say *yes* to avoid dealing with another's reaction to your *no*, you're creating a pattern based on an untruth. This pattern becomes how you operate and who you are without even knowing it. As a breeder of the *yes*, you disempower others as you constantly bail them out with your willingness. And absolutely, a piece of you gets bitter about it later. That's more of the empty Cup talking.

A while back, I had the honor of giving to a stranger and witnessing her ability to receive with grace was such a joy. A business group of women desired to gather for their own private mini-retreat, which I created with their needs in mind. After the date was set, one of the women emailed me to say she had a financial hiccup that month and would not be able to attend the retreat. Her email was written with authentic disappointment, and she wasn't blowing me off in not being able to attend.

I was called to reach out and offer her the retreat at no cost. When I told her who I was and why I was calling, she was speechless. I told her she was not alone in her moment of financial struggle and that receiving can be charged with many feelings, but I was doing this because I wanted to as I, too, have been the receiver of a similar gift. She accepted with tears, gratitude, and a pure heart.

Her openness to accept so graciously made me wish she could teach that to the rest of the world. Even though, in this case, I was the giver, I received so much by having her join us for the retreat.

I know you, too, can trace the circle in your life of giving and receiving. That's how it is with giving—everyone gains, whether it's tangible or not. Leave pride for another day and accept the invitation to be part of a beautiful dance. Pride can block you as you turn away gifts. **Receiving is an art that**

allows the giver to dance and sing. To receive from another is about accepting a gift. Think of all the times someone has offered their time, their shoulder, their help, or their love and, in return, you have said, "No, thanks. I'm good." It's like returning a present before you even unwrap it. Now, you get to have a different answer, one that supports both of you. One big fat circle of giving and receiving, receiving and giving.

REFILL REFLECTION:

- Where in your life are you closed to receiving?
- The next time you are offered a gift, offer of help, or a compliment, will you be willing to receive it with grace?
- Even if you are uncomfortable, be cognizant that someone's offering of time, help, act of service, or gift of love is in need of a recipient.
- You know how you feel after giving. Imagine that for the other person as you receive.
- Fill your Cup.

SIP 45.

UNEXPECTED GIFTS

———

Your lesson and gift are always right in front of you; only you can receive and open it.

"Hi, Georgia."

I was already late. I had to rush into the grocery store to buy an onion and a loaf of bread. That's when I saw her. I didn't know this other mom very well but well enough that I *had* to say hello.

"Oh, hi. I didn't see you there."

I bit my lip; I could have avoided this conversation.

It's my nature to say hello. I don't want anyone to feel ignored because being ignored doesn't feel good. I genuinely want to acknowledge others no matter how hasty and hurried I am in the moment.

Georgia proceeded to share a struggle she was having with her kiddo. She wanted to talk. I wanted to flee. I had moments to spare in my overscheduled day. I took a big sigh.

"I'm sorry she's struggling."

I let go of being in a rush. I connected to my feet, firmly planted on the checkered tile floor. I listened. My heart softened. She wanted to be heard. That's all any of us truly want.

Even with a listening ear and a softened heart, I became very aware of the time.

"This is a hard thing to watch our children suffer. I wish I could talk longer, but I'm running late."

It was like Georgia woke out of a trance. "Oh, I talked your ear off. Thank you for listening."

"You're welcome. I get what you're going through. This challenge she is facing will get easier. Your daughter isn't alone; other kids are struggling."

I then dashed to the bread section, all hot and bothered at myself for saying hello. An internal conflicting duality was rumbling within me. I truly would have liked to listen longer, and I was mad at myself for needing to say hello to everyone.

By the time I was out the door with my bread and onion and driving to my next stop, another light bulb went off. This one was not full of dualistic thinking. Running into her was a gift. The words I spoke to her became **the reminder I needed**. Being late was worth it. She needed to be heard. I needed to be reminded. As if one lesson a day isn't enough, when I got home, my husband had been to the store. He, too, had purchased onions. An entire bag of them and two loaves of bread.

I apparently didn't have to go to the store. Hmmm. If I had stepped off the crazy treadmill and checked in with my husband and, most importantly, checked in with myself—*Do I need to cram in going to the store now? Can I ask for help?*—I would not have made the assumption that I had to be the one to go the store. I could've used those minutes to **catch my breath before my next task**. As a mom, I take on the belief that I am the only one doing it all. I end up missing the help and offers of support. I get overloaded because I add one more task as naturally as tossing gum into the grocery cart. When I slow down and check in with myself, I'm not draining the tank, I'm leaving more fuel in it.

That day, I was empty from insisting on doing so much in a short amount of time. I was empty from reaching out to another person, trying to be everything for everyone. Luckily, that turned into a blessing. And that is how it can go, empty to full, back to empty, and full later on. All of it a blessing. A learning for tomorrow.

Where do you fit into this scenario? Would a pause be helpful on a day full of go-go-go? Do you have the urge to help everyone and be everywhere at once? Tune in. Notice your assumptions and tendency to cramming in everything. Lessons and gifts.

REFILL REFLECTION:

- Keep a journal on your bedside table or a notebook in your purse, and jot down your lesson or gift of each day.
- When you have a lot going on it can be natural to keep adding to it. Stop and ask yourself, "Do I really need to do this now?"

- Get in the practice of listening to all parts of you, not only your head.
- Notice what blessing shows up when you let go of doing more.
- Fill your Cup.

FORGOTTEN MUG ON THE WINDOWSILL

———

*I'll go ahead and put your cup of tea
on the windowsill with all the others.*

—MY LOVELY, SMART-ASS HUSBAND

I like my coffee or tea piping hot. Besides tasting better, I like the warmth and comfort it provides when holding it between my hands. There was a time, a long period of time, when I would have the intention of sitting down with my cup of steaming hot goodness to actually drink it. Squirrel. In my lofty fantasies, I would not only be drinking the entire cup before it got cold, but I would also be reading a book. A woman can dream.

What usually ended up happening is I would put the teacup above the kitchen sink on the windowsill and proceed to get distracted: a kid needed something, I checked my phone, the dog needed to be let out, the dryer beeped, the doorbell rang, or I forgot all about the tea until I reflected how nice it would be to sit down for a minute.

I'd put on the kettle, make a new cup, and be reminded some-time later in the day by my husband of all the collected cups of half-drunk cold tea from my desk, the laundry room, the fireplace mantel, or often in the bathroom. It got to the point where he would tease me regularly.

"Honey, your hot water is ready. Should I pour it over your tea bag and put it somewhere where you can't find it?"

"Ha, you're hilarious."

What made me madder than a hornet was the truth in his loving mockery. I **sought the simple comfort of stillness, and yet I didn't make it a priority** and allow myself to receive it. Dryers can beep, doorbells can ring, phone messages can wait. I made those other things a priority, dismissing my hankering for solitude that a cup of tea and a chair can offer.

This is one place the F word can come in. Not that one. The other one. **Forgive.**

I had to forgive myself for not making myself a priority. I had to understand why and make new habits. I had to get in the practice, as it doesn't come naturally to put myself first. I had to forgive my husband for being so good at pouring and drinking his entire cup of coffee while it was hot and making it to his weekly soccer games. He was setting a great example; he was modeling what I wanted. Hubby would come home from work and say, "I need a ten-minute sports update, and then I'll help with dinner."

The ten minutes he gave himself to receive the fuel that meant something to him was the same amount of time I was abandoning on the mantel or bookshelf. He makes his needs a priority and shows up to his family 100 percent.

My family wouldn't have minded, shriveled up in a corner, or been permanently damaged if I opened a book and read a chapter while sipping my hot Earl Grey with a splash of half-and-half. They would have liked me better, I tell myself, because I would've liked myself more.

Where are you leaving your needs forgotten on the windowsill?

REFILL REFLECTION:

- Figure out what you like, want, and desire.
- Make it a priority.
- Forgive yourself for not giving yourself the nurturing you give others.
- Forgive others for knowing how to take care of themselves.
- Nurture yourself.
- Fill your Cup.

TEARS ON THE FIELD

———

As a young girl, my grandmother told me that when you cry you don't have to pee as much. As an adult crier who is constantly wetting my pants, I know this is not true. What I do know is that tears are a visit from Holy Spirit, a divine gift of strength, an energy release, and a necessary conduit of grace.

Our nine-year-old son came limping off the field of his sister's soccer practice. He was invited to participate with their team, as were other younger siblings. He was crying. He was favoring his hip again as he had been off and on at his own soccer practices. I let him catch his breath and asked him to tell me about the pain. Bent down to his level, he slowly told me about the pinching and ache.

A father behind me hollered,

"Stop crying. You're okay."

I held up my index finger to indicate to the father to hold that thought for a moment. This man was often giving his opinion on the sidelines, and we were familiar enough with each other for me to hush him with a hand gesture. As I continued to listen to my son, the sideline commentary continued, and the man said one more thing to him about crying. Before I could give him a different finger to silence his chatter, my son ran across the track and up the hill, seeking solace behind the safety of a tree.

Knowing he was embarrassed, physically and emotionally uncomfortable, and needing space from all of the onlookers and the attention this man was giving him, I turned to the dad.

"You know what the problem with society is?"

Giving him no time to respond, I continued,

"Society doesn't think boys should cry."

"Boys shouldn't cry," he began and thus continued our discussion.

As we debated the right and wrong of male tears, moms walked behind the man giving me secretive thumbs up, and dads slowly stepped further and further away. For me, it wasn't a conversation about protecting my son. It was out of a **deep-rooted belief that boys throughout history have received the short end of the stick and have shouldered the burden of hiding their tears and masking their feelings**.

As we calmly articulated our personal beliefs, the father's daughter came off the soccer field in tears herself as she had gotten hurt on the field. Daddy didn't hesitate to console. I bit my lip as his daughter, two years older than my son, could let it all out and received only compassion, and not condemnation, from her father. The irony was not lost on me as I met my son on the hill and offered a hug. He hugged me back.

Society has its view on crying and so do individuals. You come to your opinions organically from personal experience. You're influenced by the views and pressures of others. The dad on the sidelines was raised to believe boys shouldn't cry but was very comfortable with the tears from his daughter. Such a cloudy line. I have been a crier my whole life, raised by a father who cried every day and a mother who never showed her tears.

The reasons for my tears as a youngster and later as a young adult were not always obvious. I would cry out of left field, over nothing particular. **Tears were my expression of anger, joy, overwhelm, delight, confusion, or fear**. The tears came unexpectedly when I was alone or in the middle of a crowd. I have since learned these were unprocessed emotions triggered by what at the time seemed like an unrelated event.

This natural wiring to cry linked me deeply to my dad, the man who spent my entire life openly shedding his tears, until he died when I was thirty-four years old. Dad cried alone in his room or sitting with me on a park bench, eating pie across the table from me at Denny's, or talking to me on the phone, and like me, he had no control over hitting the off switch. His tears flowed like a deep river that has been undammed. Chalking it up to his mental illness, I didn't know until years later that this ability to cry whenever and wherever was not only one of his characteristics I inherited but was also a gift. For that is how I view tears after my years of experiencing them: **a holy gift coming in for a visit**.

Tears are a release; pent-up energy on a mission to get up and out of you. As you stuff them down or tell your child to stuff them down, that emotion is going deeper both physically and unconsciously into the body. I believe this will fester and find a way out somehow—either through illness or an explosion of emotion. I'm not a doctor and only occasionally pretend to be one, but anyone can notice the difference you feel after crying. Notice how you can get a cold after storing up stress. **Emotion needs a place to go.**

With one parent as the crier, Mom balanced out Dad's tears by showing up as the opposite. Raised by German parents herself, crying wasn't something you did, so she would tell me to stop crying, that I cried too much, and later as an adult, she suggested I try therapy for all those tears. She wasn't mean about it; it was what she knew and the unfamiliarity of crying made her uncomfortable, especially when I was unable to offer an explanation for the tears.

When you're raised one way your beliefs get formed without even questioning them. For her tears were to be shed in privacy as they were a sign of weakness, an expression of vulnerability. Years later, in my forties, this compassion and understanding I had for tears would come full circle for my mother when she was finally ready to cry.

After my stepfather's fall from a ladder, he became dependent on my mother for everything. She would call me during breaks from caring for him, surprising herself with her tears. Tears of frustration, sadness, loss, fear, joy, and especially the tears without a clear thread to their root cause are an experience of **energy moving through us. An opening for Spirit.**

What about you? Do you tear up fast and after that release of emotion feel cleansed, lighter, and realigned? All is okay in the world again as you breathe evenly. It's not unusual for my clients cry during our life coaching sessions and all of them who do quickly apologize. Only once.

I make it quite clear that sorry is not allowed as I give them space to let the tears flow. In the work I do it's an honor to witness someone's tears and to me it is a **true sign of their strength**. As I witnessed my father, my son, and later my mother shed tears, I can't think of a greater gift. They trust me enough to show their emotion and they surrender to what needs to take place.

If you are one of those who expresses embarrassment and regret over your crying, please consider letting tears be what they are—tears. A form of expression. Would you tell a singer not to sing? Would you ask a dancer to stop dancing? Tears are an expression that needs to be let out of its cage, honored, and recognized as strength and power. **To cry is to stand in grace, no matter how messy it looks and feels.**

You don't have to fix the one in front of you crying. Be still and then ask later if they need anything from you. Give the hug if they ask for it, but know there is comfort in your stillness, as it gives them permission to release. You don't need to offer a tissue. They can get one if they need it, and remember, there is always a shirtsleeve. There is great healing power in a good cry. Despite my grandmother's mythological advice, you will still have to pee, but you will definitely have more spaciousness inside of you.

REFILL REFLECTION:

- I invite you to be curious about your relationship with tears and crying.
- How can you honor your tears or someone else's simply by letting them flow?
- If your opinion of crying encourages you or another to stuff your tears, be embarrassed, or hide them, what if you recognized tears as energy that needs to simply get out of your body?
- What if you didn't see crying as a weakness but as a strength?
- Fill your Cup.

SIP 48.

YES OR NO

———

Listen, are you at capacity?

Your gut doesn't lie.

If you don't have a **relationship with your intuition**, here is your invitation to begin. When you can listen, believe, trust, and follow it, your Cup will be full.

The line between receiving a nudge and tuning into your intuition is a blurry one. Possibly coming from Spirit. Possibly coming from your Cup. Let's not get stuck on labels but rather know that both are on your side, are rooting for you, and are soft, gentle, encouraging, and sound like you—wise you.

When I am making a decision using my gut, I shut out the other voices. This intuitive, all-knowing voice takes practice of listening to and trusting if you are not familiar with relying on its guidance. Ask the question with your feet on the ground, and yes, we talked about this in "Sip 22." I will talk about it again, right now, expanding on the concept of intuition. Your intuition knows without a long list of reasons or a lengthy explanation. It requires listening to your body and how it feels with your decision. It's a yes without a full diagram of why or it's a no without going into detail. The **more you rely on your intuition, the more you can trust it**.

Another important factor to consider is your bandwidth. Meaning, do you have the time, resources, energy, and desire when you are deciding to say yes or no to something.

My mother told me once when my kids were young, "Saying yes to volunteer must be something you're genuinely excited about."

And this comes from the woman who at ninety-one years old volunteers every week to at least three different organizations. She teaches kids to read at her local elementary school, makes meals for the homeless, knits scarves, collects signatures, offers communion, and the list goes on, generously giving of her time and energy. When the volunteer commitment is no longer feeding her, she moves on without guilt or shame, trusting that her time is up and it is someone else's time to fill that need.

When asking if you have the bandwidth to do something knowing full well that *no* would be a better answer, your reluctant *yes* carries clues that either your intuition is saying *Don't do it* or you are *at capacity*. **You feel it, so trust it.** If you say *no* from the very start, you are not only honoring your intuition and bandwidth, but you are also setting **healthy boundaries** and not giving any false expectations.

When asked by another to do something and your *yes* feels right, you are setting yourself up for success.

Always **check in with yourself and consider if you have the bandwidth** or not. Your intuition is a trusted resource for your answer, and the hard part is listening to and trusting it because you let the opinions of others control your decision-making. As you continue to practice stillness, get quiet, and give yourself moments throughout the day to only be and not do, you are creating more space for your intuition to develop, strengthen, and grow.

TIPS TO TRUST WHEN CONSIDERING YOUR BANDWIDTH CAPACITY:

- Consider if you have the physical time and energy involved to add this to your schedule.
- Are you in the right mental state to take this on?
- Is the greater good most benefitted by your *yes* or by your *no*?

TIPS TO HONOR WHEN CONSULTING YOUR INTUITION:

- Consult your emotions on this. Will the emotions that come from doing this activity, responsibility, or task serve you positively?
- What feels better?
- Is the greater good most benefitted by your *yes* or by your *no*?

When a girlfriend complains to you about having too much on her plate, you get it as you empathize with her situation and encourage her to let something go. Why is it so much easier to be compassionate to a friend than it is to yourself? You must value your bandwidth, letting go of comparison, omitting perfection, and embracing a loving response. Saying *no* is actually saying *yes* to everyone, including you. You are recognizing what is best today, in the present moment, making yourself a priority, not your ego or someone else's plan, and you **understand your limits**. You are saying *yes* because it is healthy for your body, mind, and spirit.

Honor the wisdom of your gut. She knows if you have the space for more and she isn't judging when you're at capacity—she's respecting your bandwidth.

REFILL REFLECTION:

- Begin each day checking in with your time and energy before filling up your agenda.
- Aware of what is already scheduled and what needs to be honored, tune in to your physical, mental, emotional, and spiritual capacity.
- Is your *no* and *yes* in alignment with how you are in this moment?
- Use the tips in this Sip to decide whether a *yes* or *no* is needed when deciding on taking on something new.
- Give yourself permission to say *no*, remembering that it is for the greater good of all.
- Fill your Cup.

SIP 49.

YOU'RE NOT ALONE

You're not meant to stand alone.

Carrying my screaming two-year-old son out of the grocery store, a stranger got me out the door and to my car. What feels like a hundred years ago now, as my son was having a meltdown in the checkout line, this woman I had never seen before met my tear-filled eyes. Too exhausted to look away, I received her wordless love and strength. She didn't say anything as she carried the grocery bag to my car, gave me a warm deep gaze, and went on her way. Her act of kindness got me home without falling apart in the parking lot.

Simple interactions of love, support, care, kindness, and connection carry a lot of weight.

There are the tears I have shared with Kaiti, Kristal, Karen, Angela, Annie, Lisa, or Liz over tea, coffee, wine, or vodka—standing in my kitchen, at Starbucks, or out to dinner. Then there is the laughter on the phone, in the parking lot, during a long walk, creating art, or out of town for the weekend together shared with Andie, Erika, Linda, Marcia, Mary, or Shelly. The venting, listening, connection, and support received by Dana, Laura, Lauren, Sonya, and countless other girlfriends have carried me when I could barely get up on my two feet. Affirmation and acceptance met with advice, empathy, or a hug and the reminder I'm not alone are all gifts of grace.

Gifts of grace that carry a lot of weight, which I must choose to receive.

If you can't circle yourself with a big community, make a couple of good friends or at least one. Find your peeps outside of your family to hold your hand, laugh, and cry with you and remind you that you're so many things. Beyond being mother and CEO of your family, you are friend, partner, community organizer, party girl, cheerleader, cherished daughter, and loyal sister who shows up when needed.

You are the one offering levity, perspective, and creativity at a boring meeting or showing up to book club even when you haven't read the book. You're the one who unites, organizes, plans, creates, shuffles it all, remembers to make the appointments, call ahead, ask the questions that matter, put dinner on the table, have the sex talk, and provide everyone in the family with clean underwear. You're the one who everyone can cry with and who, at the end of the day, will remind you that **you matter, regardless of what you have accomplished**.

You must, if you aren't already, **accept help**. Help from your partner, family, and friends. When you stop being stuck in your ways and insistent that you are the only one, you'll notice a shift. People will show up. Help will be at your feet. You won't be the only one carrying the mother lode.

Not only do you get to ask for help, but you also get to receive it. You forgot this because you may have not been taught it. As the queen of the mothership, remember all queens have help. If help doesn't come in the form of a live-in partner or parent, it's time to get creative. Get over yourself and recognize that it is a **symptom of strength to ask for help** and to know when enough is enough. You can't do it all. Throw any appearance of how you think it *should* look out the window and forge your own trail with helping hands along the way as you leave perfection at the curbside. Remember *should* got tossed out of your vocabulary back in "Sip 23" and *guilt* in "Sip 24."

Hello? Are you listening? **Please know this: You matter**, even when your children tell you they hate you, your boss ignores your ideas, your spouse fails to buy your asked-for tampons, or your sibling never calls. Never forget that you're needed, not only by what you do and bring to the table but by who you be. Who you *be* and how you *be* isn't about what you do and accomplish. **You are an energy of love and light.** Therefore, the care of your soul is required. You're necessary, even when they forget to say thank you and when they aren't listening to a word you're saying.

You need reserves in your tank to have the stamina, wherewithal, fortitude, and grace to be the provider, nurturer, and beautiful woman that you are, and this means asking for help and leaning on others for support. When you accept the reality of needing others' help, your Cup now has a saucer. This foundation of love and support may be Spirit for some, friends and family for others, and often the occasional stranger. Regardless of their titles, they're available for you as long as you're **willing to ask and receive**.

REFILL REFLECTION:

- Notice where you can accept help, delegate, or ask for a hand.
- Practice letting go of doing it all and see who shows up to assist.
- Asking for help often takes greater strength than doing it yourself.
- Fill your Cup.

SIP 50.

HELICOPTER

—

Hearing anything else is hard
when a helicopter is overhead.

I was eighteen years old, sitting in the back of a helicopter. My best friend, her seafood-company-owning dad, and the pilot were in the cockpit. We communicated through a microphone connected to large headphones, as it was incredibly loud. I quickly learned we had to land miles from the fish processing plant where my friend and I had been working all summer in the Aleutian Islands in Alaska on the island of Akutan.

We had been exploring the beauty of the islands from a bird's eye view and were headed back to the plant. Apparently, helicopters have small gas tanks. When there is heavy fog, it can be easy to overshoot your destination. A risk my friend's dad and the pilot didn't want to take. We landed on the island of Unimak and slept on the floor of an abandoned lighthouse.

Helicopters are efficient and powerful and can mess up a good hair day in a flash. If you aren't familiar with flying in a helicopter, you may be familiar with the not so popular term but ever popular parenting method: *helicopter parenting*. A parent with this parenting style aims to keep a close eye on their children, in the hopes of shielding them from pain and struggle and to ensure their success, ranging from playing on the jungle gym to applying for college. Their constant involvement takes on the hovering characteristic of the small aircraft. This at times excessive attention to the actions and inactions of our children can have a variety of results.

I'm guilty of the hover.

Here's what it has resulted in: thousands of arguments, yelling matches, child not trusting me, child not figuring it out on their own, resulting in feeling unprepared in life, annoyance, frustration, and anger.

Before you hover, get clear why you're hovering. Is it because you're afraid they will mess up, not succeed, or learn the lesson you had to learn the hard way? Or is it for your own personal controlling comfort—not yet ready to let go and allow them to do for themselves and, most importantly, to *be* themselves?

If we know why we're doing something, then the action isn't always necessary. **With understanding comes compassion.**

Our daughter never gave me an opportunity to hover.

"Mom, when I need your help, I will ask."

This became clear very early in her life. She does ask for help from her dad and me, very rarely, but those times are red-letter days.

"Dad, how do I file my taxes?"

"Mom, what should I do with this uncomfortable friend situation?"

We have built trust with her by trusting her first. A stumble and lesson are part of the process. You must know by now, if you have had a teen or been a teen, that most kids don't do what someone else tells them to do. The action must be their decision.

I honestly didn't start eating vegetables regularly until I was in my forties. There is only one reason why: my mom always told me to. I told myself I didn't like vegetables at all because a very long time ago that's all my mom talked about, and resisting her wisdom was easier than eating a carrot.

Hovering around our son was easy, and the reason is unfair. He's a boy. A boy who happens to have come into the world wired sensitive, and I wanted to protect him like he was a delicate egg. The best way to protect him, however, was to let him crack and allow him to fall out of the nest. This has prepared him far more than holding his hand.

Our children have different needs and thrive in multifarious ways.

Before You Start Your Helicopter Engine, Ask a Question:

What do you need from me?

How can I best support you?

What needs to happen for you to get the dishes done by 7 p.m.?

How can I help?

I'm concerned you won't meet the deadline; do I need to help or stay out of your way?

I'm getting nervous because of the time; do you need any assistance from me?

Back on the island of Akutan in 1986, it took twelve hours before anyone picked up our radio signal. Eventually, we were able to land the helicopter on a fishing vessel and make our way back home. If we hadn't been lost, we wouldn't have had the experience of falling asleep on rocks and waking to hundreds of seals napping next to us. We wouldn't have learned how to open a can of beans without a can opener, and we wouldn't have this great story to tell our grandchildren.

I invite you to **ask questions** before revving your engine. Know why you are hellbent on going into the fog. And please remember your gas tank can only hold so much.

REFILL REFLECTION:

- Get clear on your intention.
- Ask the question.
- Build trust.
- Remember, being lost is where the learning comes in.
- Fill your Cup.

SIP 51.

ART PROJECT

Anger is not the bad guy.
Anger is the teacher.

Seventeen journal pages. Forty-five minutes. Three pencils.

Many years ago, after a long day, I soaked in the bath, hoping my sadness would dissolve with the Epsom salt and lavender bath bomb. It didn't, and I remembered learning in yoga class earlier that week that one, our hips are the holder of emotion, and two, anger can be an expression of suppressed sadness.

As a child anger was viewed as ugly, negative, and hurtful in my household. Anger meant a sibling was punished, Christmas was ruined, or Dad was definitely not joining us for dinner. I adorned an invisible mask that covered up my feelings so well, I didn't even know what was underneath my feelings. I created a **pattern of dancing around my own emotions**. I never learned that **there is actually a place for anger** when handled with care.

Having small children of my own led me to hiding behind a smile and deflecting my feelings, not giving space to honor what was going on inside of me. I know now, anger has a place. And anger most definitely has a lesson to unravel. If I am willing to look below the surface, get curious, and give this emotion some air, it can be one of my greatest teachers.

TUNE IN TO YOUR EMOTIONS:

- At first sign of anger, frustration, annoyance or fill-in-the-blank emotion, name it.
- Get in touch with what you're feeling and greet it by its name. Hello, Fear. Hi there, Loneliness or Anger.
- Acknowledging the emotion takes out the charged energy underneath it. Now, ask what it wants to show you, teach you, remind you, and ultimately guide you toward.

Anger doesn't have to mean flipping off the guy in traffic or yelling at your kiddo because they left their dirty socks in the living room, again. Anger can be arising within you to be a reminder that you're upset at yourself for not leaving the house earlier, and now you're encouraged to plan your time differently in the future. Perhaps the yelling is releasing steam for not feeling recognized for all you do around the house and for your family, therefore igniting a new awareness that you're the only one right now who is capable of giving yourself credit and recognition.

Thank you, dude on the highway, or thank you, dirty abandoned socks. This process is not about making anger, or any other emotion disappear, it's about looking at it with a magnifying glass, discovering the nugget, and finding the good in it as well as giving it a voice. A voice that doesn't tear everyone else down in the process.

Back to that evening after the bath, and still swimming in a mix of frustration, anger, and sadness, I decided it was time to interview my feelings and get them out of me and onto paper. This was the beginning of a very healing project. I invite you to give this a try when you have a highly charged emotion that revisits, and you want to get below the surface. See what can happen if you are the detective and interview this visitor.

TRANSFORMING ANGER INTO ART:

- Get out your journal or many sheets of blank paper.
- Grab a black ballpoint pen or lots of pencils. (I recommend pencils over a pen.)
- For the second part of this project, get colored markers, crayons, colored pencils, or paint and a black Sharpie.
- Find a quiet place.
- Light a candle and pour yourself a cup of tea.
  - Important Note: Don't sensor what you write in the apprehension of someone finding out how mad you are about something that happened in 1995. Part II will take care of your secrets being exposed. Remember, this is a transformative process—you are breaking apart the old.

PART I:

- Name the emotion and start filling the blank page by writing the following or something like it: "I'm so sad that_____."
Begin each new sentence by filling in the blank that honors the emotion that is coming up for you. "I'm so mad that _____." Keep the pen or pencil moving until you're empty. Fill the pages with whatever comes up. You'll discover not only

the recent events and emotions arising but potentially wounds of long ago may also surface.

- Trust the process. Let these feelings explode onto the page.
- Take a breath and keep going. Come back to the statement that unlocks what is buried below the surface.
- You hold emotion in your body, and you're releasing these feelings that keep coming up for you because they aren't fully expressed or uncovered.
- There is no limit to how many pages you can fill. You may break a pencil or two and need to shake out your hand from tightly gripping your writing instrument.

PART II:

- Pause if you need a break or are emotionally exhausted and need a good cry or nap.
- When you're ready for the essential piece of turning all those feelings into a work of art, grab the colored markers, crayons, pencils, or paint. Whatever will cover your words up and conceal them from the casual onlooker.
- Start coloring. Cover the pages of emotions with a rainbow of shapes, colors, and doodles.
- When the first page is completely covered and no words are showing, get out the black Sharpie.
- Take a deep breath and ask yourself, "What do I want to feel?" Tap into an emotion or value that is important to you and write that word in big letters over the colored page with your Sharpie. Choose words you desire to embody. For example, peace, prosperity, love, grace, hope, fun, abundance, clarity, and more.
- Continue with the other pages until you have turned your pages of pent-up emotion into a kaleidoscope of happiness, joy, possibility, and peace.

For me, this process, this playful yet meaningful art project, was alchemy—turning darkness and pain, suffering and anger, into illumination. The result released stuffed down emotions. No more unnecessary invisible masks. Triggers not so triggered. Flipping off strangers and yelling at loved ones no longer became my knee-jerk reaction because I named the emotion and faced it head-on.

When something bubbles up within, I invite you to interview it, connect with it, and take it to dinner. The sooner you do that you will discover what it wants to teach you, and you won't be tied to its power. Facing it takes the charged energy down a notch or two. The emotion may be showing up to take your hand and show you how to respect your time, honor your needs, or value yourself.

Transformation is not a new thought or idea: it's the breaking down and coming apart of something that has been around for a while and is no longer serving you because you were able to turn it into something else.

REFILL REFLECTION:

- Tune in to your emotions—start naming them to yourself.
  - Give it a name—Angry Agatha, Pissed-off Polly—invite it to tea, and learn what it has to teach you.
  - When this emotion comes for a visit, ask it, "What do you want me to learn?"
  - Give yourself space to create a release and, whether it's anger or another unwelcome and unpopular emotion, transform it into art.

- No more keeping everything in (for the sake of the children). It must be expressed not only for your sake but yes, for your family too. Otherwise, it will find you and hang out in your hips or another part of you.
- When we model how to express what we are feeling the people in front of us learn.
- What emotion is ready to bust out of you, to be your teacher, your art therapist, or your healer?
- Fill your Cup.

SIP 52.

RESOURCE

———

*Time is the gift that we curse at until
we learn it's not the one to blame.*

As I tell the story, "Dad always took me to the zoo. It was our thing."

We would get ice cream, hang out with the bears and tigers, and then visit again the following week. I always wore a red shirt and had my hair cut in a bob with crooked bangs. He was always happy. It was always sunny.

"Our other thing was getting ice cream at the Little Coney at the Shilshole Bay Marina."

The same woman served us soft serve. We ate it sitting on our bench. There was one boat we pretended was ours. It was always dusk. When our ice cream was finished and dripping down my chin, we held hands walking along the shore.

In reality, we lived in Seattle. Sunshine wasn't a weekly occurrence, and my dad was severely depressed most of my life, up until the day he died when I was thirty-four years old. With his perilous depression, mental illness, and hospitalizations, it wasn't likely that we went more than once to these places. I don't think I owned more than one red shirt, and all pictures of me reveal long hair, not short.

These were my stories. My single **memories strung like pearls giving me connection** to the most important person in my life. When my children started doing something similar, I clued into how memory might work. It takes a piece of truth and weaves an important tale. My tale.

Sitting at dinner recently when our daughter was home from college, she and her brother began stringing their own pearls.

"Remember how we always went to the coast every summer?"

"Yes, and do you remember how we always stopped at that one place for milkshakes?"

It wasn't every summer, and it was once for the milkshakes. Did it matter? I bit my lip. No need to correct them. It didn't matter.

Similar perhaps to me hanging on to the zoo and marina as experiences that happened regularly, these fragments of time—less than a couple of hours out of life—hold the weight of eternity. I did the calculator math. For me, that's over 482,120.1 hours in my fifty-five years. A couple of hours leaving an imprint of love and worthiness not only on my memory but also on my heart.

Time is the biggest gift. You give it to others when you listen to your teen's struggles with a friend, your partner vent about their job, or the hand you hold when a loved one is dying. We have these moments, sands of time running down the hourglass, and we don't get them back. But they can stay with us for a lifetime. The impact they leave carries into perpetuity. Penetrating our beliefs, connections, experiences, and personal reality.

The gift you can't hold in your hand, but you most definitely feel in your heart. Whether it's a handwritten note, a call I make, or attention I give to the person in front of me, it's the thing I want to share. When a friend takes their time to sit down and share a meal with me, listen to my challenges, or make me a piece of art with their hands, I feel seen. I feel loved. And that, to me, is the best gift anyone could ask for.

Time is also the thing many of us want more of, especially at the end of a hard day. We want to start over, begin again, or go to sleep and erase it all. **Unless we choose to slow down,** these moments are all we have, and the fast-paced world we live in will cloud the poignant beauty.

On one hand, we have to keep up, got to get the taxes turned in, but on the other, there is one sunset a day. The average sunset lasts between six and eight minutes. A blink of an eye. And I personally miss them all, when I live only blocks away from a spectacular view of the horizon. I fill those minutes with doing dishes, scrolling on my phone, or catching up on email.

In moments of overwhelm, my phone is an escape. Then the next thing I know, I'm no longer on this planet. My mind elsewhere. Numerous occasions of time spent on my phone depleting me became the go-to habit when I was tired, frustrated, or distracted. Too many times this scenario woke me up to realize my relationship with my phone needed a reboot. And now, years later, I have a spot to store my phone when I'm not using it and self-imposed boundaries, so I don't get lost in mindless scrolling.

The quickest way for me to get depleted is to get lost in social media feeds that leave me uninspired, jealous, overwhelmed, bored, and in a state of comparison and confusion. That's when it is necessary to stop and ask, *How do I want to spend my time? Am I using my time in a way that empties or fulfills?*

One memory I hope our children will carry with them forever is the summer ritual they each have, not necessarily together, typically on their own to walk or drive five blocks away to watch the sun disappear behind the Olympic mountains. They each have done this on many occasions. This inspires me to slow down and reminds me to choose intentionally and deliberately like a string of pearls.

You give your time. That is the most precious resource anyone can give. You set your day around caring for others. In doing so, you wait until there is time for yourself. As you see it, it will happen later because right now there isn't enough time. **What if you gave your time *and* receive its gift?** I invite you not to wait and to look at time differently, like a precious jewel.

Time is all you have, and the memory of how you spend it is priceless.

REFILL REFLECTION:

- Let's say you are awake sixteen hours on average, each day. How much time do you want to spend that is unplanned, spacious, and without an agenda?
- What if you started with the time it typically takes the sun to set?
  - Begin with six minutes of connection and timelessness, stringing together your own strand of pearls.
- Notice the teachers who inspire you on how you want to spend your time.
- Do you want to restructure your relationship with your phone?
  - Give yourself parameters.
  - Keep your phone in a designated spot.
  - Turn off the sound and/or notifications on your phone.
  - Give yourself a set amount of time you want to spend on social media.
    - Stick to it.
    - Create rules that work for you.
- Fill your Cup.

BE ONE

———

All issues root in disconnection.

"There is no 'I' in team."

Years ago, I worked with a local high school girls basketball team at the start of each season to gain clarity about their vision, goals, and focus. One season I was called in before playoffs as there was dissension among the ranks. No longer finding their rhythm as one, they were lost in their own heads, concerned about their individual achievements. Despite finishing their regular season undefeated, they had forgotten what one of their former coaches had taught them.

Coach Sonya Elliot always said, "There is no 'I' in team."

Some of the players had given up because of who they were set to play next: a tough team, the previous year's state champs. No longer on the same page, the **voices of naysayers, mostly their parents, were getting in their heads.**

"Hang 'em up; it's been a good season."

One half of the team buying into the predicted defeat and the other not ready to give up. The big game scheduled in three days was their opportunity to come together. For cohesion to be restored they had to find one common thread. It was time to work as one and play ball as a group, not individuals. It was time to share the responsibility as a whole, like any family unit.

I spoke with the team captain first.

"What needs to happen?" I asked the six-foot-six center.

"We need to figure out what can bring us together."

We gathered the team in the locker room. Yep, smells as bad as a boys'.

"We need a word or phrase that we can say on the court when everything is falling apart."

As they spoke out possible ideas, I filled the whiteboard. They settled on their unanimous vote.

"Be one."

"Okay, this is great. What are the qualities needed to 'be one'?"

"Strength."

"Trust."

"Unity."

"Confidence."

"Communication."

Their answers flew at me faster than a hard pass with only seconds on the shot clock. My hand couldn't keep up with their wisdom.

"Let's make a phrase we can chant on the court that means all these things and especially commitment and strength."

"We have to rely on each other."

This team was remembering who they were at the beginning of the season.

"I got it," said one of the quieter players. "Show up."

On cue, like they had met before and rehearsed their answer, they responded,

"We are one."

That was it. It was what they needed. Similar to a family struggling, conflict in the air, this team found the elements a family needs: commitment, communication, confidence, reliability, strength, trust, and unity. They came up with a plan to embody and embrace these characteristics. And when things got messy on the court, one of the five would shout their created come-together phrase.

"Show up."

The entire team, on and off the court, would respond, "We are one."

Their plan came together. Remembering what filled the locker room whiteboard, they went on to be district champs that season.

Desperate times call for cooperation. All issues invite coming together. Getting on the same page as a team, as a parent with children, or in any relationship involves a belief in commitment. You have to **decide if you're committed to your doubt or your faith**. Whichever one you tie yourself to wins.

Like on the basketball team, each player had a gift, whether it was making three-pointers or killer defense—every member of a family has gifts, and it's no accident that you are all together. **Recognize, honor, and utilize the gifts** of all your players. Whether it's getting out the door for school, borrowing the car when the oldest child turns sixteen, helping out around the house, or choosing a college for next year.

Your family is your team, no matter the ages. Head coach, that's you, must find your breath, remove doubt, connect to yourself, and unite your team. Before you yell, tie yourself to faith—faith in you all rising above the chaos, faith in unity. Connect to your breath and best self—deflating that urge to scream. **Find that common thread** that matters to each of you, and utilize the gifts of all. Don't give up before the season is over, despite the naysayers.

REFILL REFLECTION:

- You're probably not headed to a state basketball championship, but where are there other opportunities close to your heart that involve others?
- Is it time to get on the same page?
- Is it time for a family circle?
  - Gather up.
  - Connect with everyone's values.
  - Make a plan.
  - Allow leadership to rotate.
  - Lighting a candle never hurts.
  - Honor the voices, and remember you are a unit.
- Show up.
- Be a team.
- Fill your Cup.

SIP 54.

BOOKEND

———

*Like a bookend holds up a stack of
books, we are better supported when
we have something to lean on.*

I have two favorite parts of any movie or book: the beginning
and the end. I'm excited about a new story, new characters,
and the possibility of what will be unveiled. If the ending
sucks, I am more than disappointed. I feel incomplete. I don't
need a happy ending; I need realistic closure.

I am the same about my day.

I wake up excited for another opportunity, curious and in
wonder about the possibility the hours will unfold. And if I
get to the end of the day without a moment to process it all,
it feels incomplete. It's like going through the drive-through
and realizing your fries are missing. You've got to park the
car, go back in, and get the best part of the meal.

Because the beginning and end of a day are my most cherished parts, I have learned that honoring them are essential.

I begin my day with something small that is important to me. What I choose to do depends on the season I am in. If I am in moving my body mode, it is a workout at Row House, physical therapy in my carpeted basement, or I roll out the yoga mat in the living room and drop into a few poses and stretches. If I'm in my spiritual season, the day begins with meditation and prayer. If my mental Cup needs filling, then I turn to my journal or open a book of poetry. It doesn't seem to matter what it is, although I have learned my spiritual and mental needs usually far outweigh my physical.

It's vital to begin with one of my rituals. I don't roll into the day; I **step into it intentionally**. When I skip this deliberate part of the morning, I end up yelling at a kid, snapping at my husband, frustrated for not showing up for myself, or completely drained by noon. I need a beginning that sets the stage for the day, much like the drawing back of the curtains on a play.

As much as I would like to spend an entire morning in my pajamas doing yoga, reading, writing, meditating, sipping tea, pulling oracle cards, getting in touch with my breath, praying, listening to music, and all the things that I enjoy doing, I don't have that luxury. I have clients waiting. Appointments to attend. Meals that need cooking and a sink to scrub.

Thankfully, through all my practices of beginning my day with something that fuels me, I have learned it only takes one thing to start the new day on purpose. I have learned that my **nonnegotiable is doing something that I love** that has meaning and purpose beyond the act itself. My **nonnegotiable is showing up to myself** by the first ten minutes of the day.

If I have opened my journal, sat in meditation, or driven to Row House I have set down the first bookend to hold me up.

This brings me to the end of the day.

One of the above actions that bring me joy can easily be incorporated into the last thing I do at night. Typically, in this season, it is writing in my bedside journal and a three-minute meditation. Then, if I haven't turned out the light, I read for about ten minutes. I begin showing up to me, and I end showing up to me. That is a day where I have honored myself. And that is nonnegotiable, no matter how busy I have been or how tired I am.

Beginning and ending. Bookends. Closure. Full circle.

Is closure important to you? Do you have a simple action that feeds you as it marks the beginning and ending of each day? Wouldn't it be nice to allow some sort of holding yourself up that makes sense to you rather than rolling into one day and out of the next without acknowledgment or completion?

There will be seasons when your beginnings and endings have more to it and take more time and others where bookending your day looks like one breath, one gratitude, or one kiss. I invite you to play around with starting your day with an action for yourself, before you let the dog out if possible. Standing in the grass and waking to the day can be a beautiful opening to your first act.

Some days, exhaustion will take precedence over reading a chapter of a book. I still invite you to pick something simple that has meaning. It is often **the smallest of acts that have the biggest impact**.

REFILL REFLECTION:

- What are some thoughts you have around one nonnegotiable for the beginning and end of your day?
- Brushing your teeth doesn't count unless you incorporate that action with checking in with yourself. Be mindful of your gratitude. One thankful thought for each tooth you brush.
- Taking your dog outside counts if there is something in it for you.
- Begin simple.
  - Start with trying this out for three days out of one week.
  - Set yourself up for success.
  - If bookending your day with reading, leave the book visible.
  - If bookending your day with a one-minute breath practice, put a sticky note visible to remind you.
- Fill your Cup.

SIP 55.

FILL YOUR CUP

---

*You are the holder, the pourer, and
the drinker of your Cup.*

When I was that little girl, behind my closed bedroom door, my family couldn't reach me. My dad's sadness, my mom's fear, my siblings' anger, confusion, and overwhelm, all that had nothing to do with me. I found my own peace.

Playing with my stuffed animals, lost in a book, looking out the window in my wistful fantasy world, I was fine. Perfectly fine. I didn't know it then, but I was connected to the best version of me. No friend, no parent, no nothing could rock my boat or stand in my way. I found the Divinity within by trusting it was there without even seeing it. Without even knowing what it was. And that is what I can tell you. **You hold the key to filling up your Cup.**

It's not easy. The unlocking takes practice, patience, and persistence. Please look at how far you have come. You have raised and taken care of so many people while continuing to develop, figure out, and care for yourself. It is you who must whisper *I love you* until your bones soften and your heart breaks open.

No one else's words, touch, or actions will heal your pain or fill your emptiness. Yes, the love and kindness from another adds to your self-love and, on a good day or in a ripe season, can overflow your Cup. Without your own loving, the love, compassion, and care of others won't stay in the Cup. There will be nothing for it to stick to. **Your self-love is the foundation for you to receive.** The missing puzzle piece in a complex life.

You must practice looking within. All the outside stuff is temporary, bandages to get you by until the next thing comes along. Until you can stand in front of the mirror accepting yourself as is—whole and complete, more than enough—you will continue to search for how to fill your empty Cup.

Bravo for holding out your Cup, not comparing it to anyone else's, and pouring what you need when you need it.

You are not alone. Remember the circle you are standing in? Look to your warriors, healers, and teachers and, most importantly, look in the mirror. Pull out your tool belt. Trust the unfolding and be your truth. Your visionary is waiting for you, wanting to hold your hand.

REFILL REFLECTION:

- Will you trust your intuition?
- Will you ask for help?
- Will you delegate?
- Will you receive support?
- Will you receive the invitation to believe yourself?
- How will you fill your Cup?

WEAVING IT ALL TOGETHER

---

*The great thing about spinning out
of control is that it becomes your
teacher, your friend, and your guide
to lead you off the roller coaster.*

Those in her wake feel the wrath
Spun out of control, she stands holding an empty Cup
All those around her caught up in the hurricane.

She got here by giving too much
Saying yes when her heart gently tried to get her attention
Her no would have filled others up, empowered them with
    new wings.

She got here by time travel
Standing in a future moment or day tripping to a time in
    the past
Basking now in awareness she knows how to avoid empty
    more often.

She honors her soul, fully aware of its guiding voice
Pauses to breathe, says *not now* and takes out *should* with
the trash
She understands the power of guilt and that it's a poor excuse.

Refusing to be a statistic writing her own manual
Owning her feelings, she explodes with beauty and grace
Releasing control, choosing her commitments wisely.

Standing in the present moment—physically, mentally, emo-
tionally, and spiritually
She comes home to herself
Discerning with all parts, she anchors to joy.

Like yin and yang, she practices what matters.
She visits church on the mountaintop
Giving thanks and praise.

Clinging to faith in herself, her life, her God
Empowering those around her she remembers to believe
She listens in the stillness and gives up judgment.

The smell of an ocean breeze or a summer rain
Bring her back to the present
As she agrees to follow her heartbeat, not the rules of others.

Her roots are strong
Receiving from her circle
Responsible for her energy and releasing what isn't hers.

Applying love
Laying down the distraction
Picking up what calls.

Time is on her side
Queen of manifesting
Lighting her candle in the dark.

Switching her perspective,
Widening the view
Rejuvenated, refilled.

Detaching from what drains
Plugging into what gives life
She expresses herself fully.

Focused on what is in front of her
Paying attention to what she can carry
Surrendering the rest.

Trusting in this thing called life
No longer ignoring or numbing
She makes herself a priority.

She inhales
Before anything else, she exhales
Then she exhales again.

REFILL REFLECTION:

- Pick a couple of the sentences above that really speak to you and make them your own.
- Practice the message.
- When the message is yours and it has become a part of you, pick up the next one calling your name.
- Fill your Cup.

CONCLUSION

———

Dear Reader,

The birth of this book began in a moment of frustration. I heard a voice. I trusted, followed, and eventually answered that voice, clueless of where it would lead me. That is my invitation to you—hear your voice, trust it, believe in it, honor it, and have faith where it will lead you. The exact year is foggy, but my best guess is I heard the voice over fourteen years ago. Be patient with yourself and the process. You are exactly where you need to be; don't rush. Everything is unfolding as it needs to.

It is never too late to heal and pull back the layers. Even though my work began earlier, I didn't face my childhood until my fifties. These things can take time and don't need to be rushed. Only noticed. There will always be more to uncover and more to heal from, and the best place to start that process is from right where you are. I avoided personal growth because I didn't know where to begin. When I finally took my own counsel, I removed blame and dug in. It's never a straight line or clean process. My parents didn't do it perfectly, nor have my husband and I, but forgiveness has been my friend—the thing to set me free.

My voice has changed considerably from when this project began, and even as I add the last words and scoop up all I want to share, I know there is so much more I want to tell you. There are so many things I have left out. There are other nuggets that I believe are important. Like life, everything has its own timing, and as I continue to unpack my learning and growth, I know you will too.

I'm excited for you to be a full participant in your life, to trust your inner wisdom as you remember to love yourself with all your heart, with both feet on the ground, and with both arms wrapped firmly around your shoulders. Replacing self-love with caring for others or raising a family didn't serve me. It took caring for others to realize that first I must care for me.

This life and all your relationships are guiding you home. Follow your own light, be anchored to your truth, trust the wisdom to teach you, and know all is well.

Thanks for playing.

Cheers, Jenny

ACKNOWLEDGMENTS

—

This book and the idea for it wouldn't have come to be if it weren't for my family. They are and continue to be my teachers. I don't want to wait until the end to celebrate my Team Family—Rob, Maggie, and Simon.

Rob, you have taught me how to be the best version of me, and I thank you for standing beside me in this crazy ride of life, collecting all my cups on the windowsill. I continue to choose you. This book has taken more than a decade, and without your belief in me and continued support, I would've given up long ago.

Maggie and Simon, you teach me every day how to not only be a better mom but also to be a better person. Thank you for being my guides in loving unconditionally.

Accountability is a great friend, and writing every Thursday with Sonya Elliott for the past fifteen years has kept me faithful to the blank page. Thank you writing partner for your friendship, tireless editing, and dedication to our passion.

Friendship doesn't have to include reading your friend's manuscript, but many of you have, cheering me on from the sidelines and inspiring me to continue: Dan Pierce and all the others whose names are blurring in my mind but not my heart, thank you.

I have an incredible pack of women (and men) who continue to support, inspire, and feed me—you know you who are. Thank you from the bottom of my heart. You listen to me when I doubt and believe in me when I have forgotten how.

Thank you, clients and retreat attendees, who shall remain nameless, but to me your faces, names, and stories are forever imprinted on my Cup.

In the early days, the editing eye of Chris Nelson was priceless. To all my teachers and editors of the craft, I bow in gratitude. I so appreciate the time and energy spent by Valerie Long, Lauren Hudspeth, and Emily Davila to be my beta readers. Your feedback is priceless. Thank you, Whitney McGruder and the entire staff at New Degree Press and Yoke and Abundance Press. What an adventure it's been. Thanks for throwing me a paddle.

And last but never least, thank you to all the moms and dads who encourage, motivate, strengthen, and inspire my own parenting, my own holding tenderly of the Cup. Especially to mine, Elizabeth and Jack, to whom I owe my life.

A huge heartfelt thank you to all who preordered their own copy of this book. Your generosity and support blow me away, and without it we wouldn't be holding this book in our hands.

With overflowing gratitude I thank: Adelaide Waters, Aleece McGlothern, Alison Forsythe, Amy Anderson, Amy Cope, Amy French, Amy Rudolf, Amy Steers, Andie Merlino, Angela Fleet, Angela Greene, Angela Reid, Ann Nicolaysen, Anne Corley, Anne Durkin, Anne Perry, Anne Weglin, Annette Miller, Annie Higgins, Anya Jepsen, Barbara Kreemer, Becky Augsberger, Beth McKillop, Betsey Beckman, Brittiony Borges, Byron Hutson, Cami MacDonald, Carrie Meek, Cathryn Booth-LaForce, Cathy Hitchcock, Cathy Long, Christina Mastrangelo, Christine Palidar, Cindy McGlothern, Cindy Ward, Claire Howes, Claudia Haon, Dan Pierce, Dana Kaefer, Dana Ross, Dawn Gramling, DeAnne Howisey, Debbie Conn, Debbie Ellingson, Debbie Sweetland, Deirdre Noonan, Donna Veenhuizen, Eden Riddell, Elizabeth Hansen, Eric Blaser, Flora Fleet, Gina Santiano, Gina Spadoni, Gretchen Gundrum, Hayden Howes, Holly Bauersfeld, Jana Claxton, Jana Johnson, Jane Hutson, Jane Kortz, Jane Seibel, Jane Summerfelt, Jane Wainwright, Janet Sjoblom, Janet Summerfelt, Janice Damon, Jenn Ott, Jennifer Herrin, Jennifer Livingston, Jenny Farrell, Jill Rose, Jodene Davis, Jody Jones, Jordan Quinn, Juliana Burzynski, Julie Jenkins, Julie Pietsch, Kaiti Grassley, Karen Recasnser, Karen Whorton, Kate Voss, Kathleen Gotti, Kathy Banak, Katie Sala, Kayce Hughlett, Kelly Malloy, Kerry Casteel, Kimithy Nagel, Kippy Depina, Kiran Robertson, Kristal Maurstad, Laura Carter, Laura Douglas, Lauren Hudspeth, Leslie Morgan, Liesl Langley, Linda Filley Bentler, Linda Pierce, Lindsay Ruf, Lisa Hagar, Liz Murphy, Lucy Chen, Marcia Alexander, Marcia Metcalf, Marie LeBaron, Marta O'Neil, Mary Edmondson, Mary Heuman, Mary Nicholls, Mary Zwaller, Mary Claire Shaughnessy, Megan Bird, Megan Riley, Melinda LeClerq, Meredith Vela, Michelle Neal, Michelle Woodbury, Nick D'Souza, Paula

Mulhauser, Pete Wilson, Robin Garboden, Rena Yong, Rene Miller, Renee Marquardt, Roxanne Topacio, Ryan Breske, Sam Lunsford, Sandi Buchanan, Shana Allen, Sarah Petersen, Sharon Brown, Sharon Richards, Shelly Hunter, Shelly Sazama, Sonja Kalbfleisch, Sonya Elliott, Stacey Crabtree, Sue Cook, Sue Kelly, Suzanne Thomsen, Taeya Lauer, Terri Burleson, Toddy Dyer, Trish Cosgrove, Wes Kalbfleisch, Willy Vancrey.

My Cup overfloweth.

APPENDIX

SIP 6

Kidd, Sue Monk. 2016. *When the Heart Waits: Spiritual Direction for Life's Sacred Questions.* San Francisco: HarperOne.

SIP 8

Ravitch, Diane. 2011. "The Senseless Death of Carol Gotbaum." *HuffPost Contributor* (blog), *The Huffington Post.* May 25, 2011. https://www.huffpost.com/entry/the-senseless-death-of-ca_b_67555.

SIP 9

Drucker, Karen. 2018. "The Power of Ritual." *Karen Drucker* (blog). September 2, 2018. https://www.karendrucker.com/2018/09/the-power-of-ritual/.

SIP 12

Stevenson, Robert Louis. 1892. *Across the Plains, with Other Memories and Essays.* Germany: Cosimo Classics.

PART 2 TRUTH

Ruiz, Don Miguel. 1997. *The Four Agreements: A Practical Guide to Personal Freedom (A Toltec Wisdom Book).* San Rafael, CA: Amber-Allen Publishing, Incorporated.

SIP 15

Ruiz, Don Miguel. 1997. *The Four Agreements: A Practical Guide to Personal Freedom (A Toltec Wisdom Book).* San Rafael, CA: Amber-Allen Publishing, Incorporated.

SIP 16

Ruiz, Don Miguel. 1997. *The Four Agreements: A Practical Guide to Personal Freedom (A Toltec Wisdom Book).* San Rafael, CA: Amber-Allen Publishing, Incorporated.

SIP 17

ArtisanNewsService. 2007. "Stuart Smalley Born From Al-Anon Meeting."
ArtisanNewsService. May 3, 2007. 01:54.
https://www.youtube.com/watch?v=3xqKkLlCfLE&t=20s.

Ruiz, Don Miguel. 1997. *The Four Agreements: A Practical Guide to Personal Freedom
(A Toltec Wisdom Book)*. San Rafael, CA: Amber-Allen Publishing, Incorporated.

SIP 18

Ruiz, Don Miguel. 1997. *The Four Agreements: A Practical Guide to Personal Freedom
(A Toltec Wisdom Book)*. San Rafael, CA: Amber-Allen Publishing, Incorporated.

SIP 25

Brown, Brené. 2012. *Daring Greatly: How the Courage to Be Vulnerable Transforms
the Way We Live, Love, Parent, and Lead*. New York City: Penguin Books.

SIP 28

Dyer, Wayne W. 2017. "Just Say 'Thank You!'" *Dr. Wayne W. Dyer* (blog). November
29, 2017.
https://www.drwaynedyer.com/blog/just-say-thank-you/.

Syrus, Publius. 2015. *The Moral Sayings of Publius Syrus, a Roman Slave: From the
Latin-Scholar's Choice Edition*. Sacramento: Creative Media Partners, LLC.

SIP 35

Pressfield, Steven. 2002. *The War of Art: Break through the Blocks and Win Your
Inner Creative Battles*. New York: Warner Books, Inc.

SIP 42

Silver, Erin. 2016. "Moms Who Want to Get Away, Get Centered Are Heading to
Retreats Just for Them." *The Washington Post*, November 29, 2016.
https://www.washingtonpost.com/news/parenting/wp/2016/11/29/retreats-for-
moms-are-everywhere-heres-why/.

SIP 44

Baldwin, Christina. 2002. *The Seven Whispers: A Spiritual Practice for Times Like
These*. Novato: New World Library.

Henri Nouwen Society. 2018. "Daring to Become Dependent." *Henri Nouwen Society*
(blog). April 4, 2018.
https://henrinouwen.org/meditations/daring-become-dependent/.

Printed in the USA
CPSIA information can be obtained
at www.ICGtesting.com
LVHW020520031023
759754LV00017B/613